EYES MADE OF SOUL

Eyes Made of Soul

The Theory and Practice of Noetic Balancing

Robert D. Waterman, EdD, LPCC

Copyright © 2010 by Robert D. Waterman, EdD, LPCC.

Library of Congress Control Number:		2010905498
ISBN:	Hardcover	978-1-4500-8686-8
	Softcover	978-1-4500-8685-1
	Ebook	978-1-4500-8687-5

All rights reserved. No part of this book may be reproduced or transmitted in any form or by any means, electronic or mechanical, including photocopying, recording, or by any information storage and retrieval system, without permission in writing from the copyright owner.

Robert Waterman
Santa Fe, New Mexico
505-466-8385
rdwnexus@gmail.com

This book was printed in the United States of America.

To order additional copies of this book, contact:
Xlibris Corporation
1-888-795-4274
www.Xlibris.com
Orders@Xlibris.com
79199

Contents

FORWARD 13

INTRODUCTION 19

Chapter One
STUDENT'S MIND 27

Chapter Two
SELF AS NOETIC FIELD 40

Chapter Three
FABRIC OF SELF 53

Chapter Four
ESSENTIAL UNDERSTANDING 74

Chapter Five
NOETIC BALANCING 94

Chapter Six
DEVELOPING STYLE 114

Chapter Seven
ZERO POINT INDEXING 140

Chapter Eight
NATURE OF IMBALANCES 151

Chapter Nine
EXPERIENCE OF NOETIC BALANCING 174

APPENDIX ONE: THE PRACTIONER MYSTIQUE 191

APPENDICE DEUX: FRANÇAIS.. 193

BIBLIOGRAPHY 197

DEDICATION

To those who understand that in the depths of their heart
lives the transformation of human kind.

Acknowledgements

With deep gratitude, we recognize the vision and dedication of Neva Dell Hunter, Ellavivian Power, John Clark McDougall, and Ralph Gordon for translating the healing of Phineus Parkhurst Quimby into what we now call Noetic Balancing.

We have never been alone. For that we give thanks to the Travelers, Avatars, Buddhas, Christs, Sahdus, Rishis, Imams, Priest, Pastors, Teachers, Shaman and Initiates who, through the ages, guided, lifted, taught and were there to show us the way.

EYES MADE OF SOUL

Consider, each moment of your life.
You breathe in and out.
You are alive.
Some moments are easy.
You respond: more clothes or less, a smile or a frown, silence or laughter, yes or no.
Then, something really humiliating and dangerous happens.
Did you respond well?
Did you measure up to your ingrained standard?
Did you get the love and nurturing that you needed?
You seem like a victim, but you actually blame yourself.
You ask yourself: Am I good enough? Lovable? Sufficient?
And you decide.

You fold your precious life force into a container of belief
        and it becomes a law inside of you.
It drops into your unconscious and emerges in the noetic field
        that fills the space around your body,
            telling you and others who you believe yourself to be,
        your story.

You wrote your story using your serial responses to each moment, each event,
        woven by each breath into a phantasmagoria
        walking down the street in its atmospheric delight,
        pretending it is a real person.

Reality shuffles itself to match your stacked deck.
Reality folds in upon itself in order to match your specifications.
Your DNA takes notes.
Your dynamic flow of life throttles itself down
        to match your selected rate.
Your perfect life form conforms to imperfection upon your decree.
I am unlovable, incapable, shameful, doomed to live out a story
        that says my role in life is to promote my servitude
          so I can belong and get what I need.
Or its corollary: I am special, self-made, destined to pluck from life and others,
            whatever I want to make me good, better, more deserving, dominant.

Your soul light gradually recedes into the darkness.
Love folds itself into the garb of an imposter.
The only reality you can see is the one reflected in the mirror of your life.
It seems so right after awhile that you forget that mirrors
       reverse images playing them back to you as if they are true.

All mirror images are reversed.
The most breath-taking world-vista imitates your soul.
So, you seek your soul by striving for images that hand you the opposite of
       your holiness.
You pile conquest upon conquest, only to want or need more.

Fulfillment is an internal moment between you and your inner light.
Discontent is your friend.
The deconstructed life is your salvation.

Sing love songs into the dark void within,
       until the soul returns and lights your way with truth.

Look through eyes made of soul.

The mirror is the gift of the universe.
Your soul is your gift to eternity.

Forward

There is change in the wind. My sense is that reality as we understanding it is changing quickly. If your nature is to draw you sense of self from your soul, these times are exciting. If you rely on a sense of self based on traditional beliefs, political power or dogmatic certainty, fear is, to varying degrees, haunting your perception of what is safe, certain or true. This book is about a transformational approach that increasingly avails the individual of the living love. The living love is the love that comes through the sense of oneself as soul and mitigates the elements of our nature that makes us prone to anger, judgment and blame as our sources of self and power.

After 40 years of evolution, the material in this book seemed settled by 2007. Then I added the chapter on Zero Point. The reality is that this material evolves as I write, so it is never ending in that sense. I have become increasingly aware of an emergent phenomenon of transformational practices that are actually forms of *noetic balancing*. Because of that, I felt the need in a recent Blog (2010) (*www.mystery-school.com*) to put this phenomenon in context, as I saw it. Continuing with that inspiration, it seems appropriate to repeat it here as a forward to the introduction to *Eyes Made of Soul*.

Seeds of Spirit: The Harvest of P. P. Quimby

The words were like keys that opened the pages of my heart. I was young. Like Paul, I wanted to be "face to face." Like John, I wanted to see the "sky open." Like Jesus, I wanted to be "one with." Like the Pentecost, I wanted to experience the "mystical wind." Ancient seeds fell on fertile soul. One day they sprouted. The sky did open and after that I could gaze into the seeming inner darkness. Images and metaphoric scriptures emerged. It seemed that the true message was for the outer word to awaken the inner ones. The "wind" of spirit spoke to me through my soul.

I began meeting people who experienced and delivered the ancient teachings in a real and tangible way. No more dogma covering the shadows of fear nor political agendas passing as inspired guidance. After my fragile beginning and many interesting discussion with people who had no experience to offer, I was meeting people who experienced spirit and could do things. Christ, to them, was real, up close and personal, in contrast to abstract, historical and dogmatic.

I met Phenius Parkhurts Quimby in Alamogordo, New Mexico. That may seem strange to say, since he allegedly passed in 1866. Trust me, things are never as they seem. That was a scientific principle for Quimby. I went to Alamogordo to study with Dr. Hunter who I met in Santa Barbara, California, in 1966. She was like a circuit rider. She traveled around the United States and parts of Canada, teaching and giving readings similar to Edgar Cayce. She went into a trance state, and an alter-ego would speak that called itself Dr. Gordon, who subsequently revealed that he was Quimby in his past life.

Dr. Hunter, John Clark McDougall, and Ellavivian Power developed an energy healing that they called Aura Balancing. When I met Dr. Hunter in Santa Barbara, I had dropped out of the University of Santa Barbara. I was overwhelmed and stuck. When my first Aura Balancing was over, my reality was entirely different. I was clear, aligned, motivated and alert. I re-enrolled and soon graduated. I had directly experienced the healing of Quimby. In my session, Dr Hunter and her colleague cleared blocks and congestion in my aura. The aura is a morphic field that surrounds and penetrates the physical body. The beliefs held in this field inform our health and mental emotional balance. The physicist, David Bohm, called the field the implicate order. Rupert Sheldrick called it the morphogenetic, or morphic, field, meaning form making field.

The process was simple. Through a prayer the practitioner aligned with the Holy Spirit (wholeness), merged fields with the client, engaged blocks and distortions detected in the field, then dissolved or balanced these aberrations. The balancing actions occurred through a spiritual action enabled by the practitioner's witness. The session ended when the field appeared light filled and felt whole, smooth and silky. The practitioner then disentangled from the client's field through a closing process. The practitioner began with an intention to serve the client, but made no promises. Jesus said, "that which you tell God in secret will be given to you openly and abundantly." That is an amazing statement. In other words, in the balancing the intention is given into the wholeness of spirit while the practitioner engages the point in the field and watches God work according to its own wisdom rather that the agenda of the practitioner. Change happens and client's heal and transform. At the time of my first experience, I was amazed. My amazement continues. Each session is a predictable mystery. The physical symptom may change and the healing is always a change of heart. That is not an excuse. It is a truth. A love filled life is the greatest healing.

One day when I was in a class with Dr. Hunter/Gordon, I looked over at her, and clear as day, there sat Quimby, for a moment, then his image was gone. From then on, I felt I had personally met the man and that I had a collegial relationship with him. Cool. I could say: "well Park (his nickname) what do you think of this?

Quimby, like quantum physicists of today, looked at "science" as everything outside of what we conventionally call science. This is the same contrast as Newtonian and Quantum Physics. These are *seeds of Sirit*. In his day, Quimby sat with his clients and explained to them that "dis-ease" was caused by beliefs that blocked and distorted the easy access to the inner Christ. He called his approach the "Science of the Christ." Once the client had reconciled their beliefs, Quimby "worked with them silently." These same steps appear in the Balancing work: merge with the client in the spirit of the Christ, give to God the intention to heal, engage the blocking beliefs and distorted energy, deconstruct, then witness and observe the transformation of the energy as information, which then informs the client's reality differently. The change in reality is often experienced as healing. The transformation is often more than expected and is frequently different than expected.

As a renewal of the healing taught by Jesus, Quimby's work is like a second seeding. Through his teaching as Dr. Hunter's alter ego, Aura Balancing developed beginning in the early 1960's. The Aura Balancing was like a third seeding. The way a seed works is that you formulate its' matrix and then plant it in human experience and release it. It grows in the collective field of the unconscious. As balancing evolved, I expanded it into Noetic Balancing. I did this because, over time, our experience revealed a much broader action than the personal aura. We were engaging a field that was the entire matrix of which the aura, as we understood it, was the immediate morphic field of the body.

More recently, those original seeds are sprouting through seemingly unrelated sources. A morphic field began with Jesus and was added to by Quimby. It is now expanding into increasingly new application through the consciousness of humanity. When we connect with this field, we can know what the field knows.

One of the more dramatic contemporary harvests is Matrixenergetics, developed by Dr. Richard Bartlet. Perhaps, I should say, continually developed by Dr. Bartlet. Essentially, he merges with the matrix—what I call the noetic field and Bohm calls the implicate order—and moves into a rapport with the client with the intention to heal often using the symptom of the client as a starting reference, notices and connects with two points on the client's physical body or in their field, drops his consciousness into the wholeness, and the reality of the client changes. Where have we seen this program before?

I would like to include one other healer in this discussion, Vianna Steible. She developed Theta Healing. Through her conversations with God, she applies the same elements. She connects with All That Is, either through merging with the matrix of going up and connecting with the field of universal love. Once connected, she places an intention with the Father-Mother God, All That Is, by stating that it is commanded that the change in condition occur. She gives thanks. Moves her awareness to witness and observes the healing occur, watching the change in reality. She continues to observe until the transformation is complete.

From the seeding of Quimby, the harvest is great. Noetic Balancing, Thetahealing and Matrixenergetics are examples that I know about that apply the essential elements of the Science of the Christ. The "silent work" as Quimby referred to it is key. Would you like to test the waters?

Be with a friend, client, or colleague. Sit or stand. Engage your connectedness and through that kinship you are in rapport with each other. With your hand, touch the frequency of this rapport. You can sense it clearly with your touch, and in the rapport of the surrounding field. Give thanks for the presence of living love. Give thanks for the presence of the Christ and Holy Spirit, if you like. Give thanks for the presence of Allah, or the Buddha consciousness, if you like. Give thanks. Realize that this is your reality and that your colleague is a mirror within that realty as you are a mirror within hers, within his. There is nothing to fix, no problem to solve. Ask your colleague to tell you their concern. This is the intention you will give to God, All That is, through your connectedness, your kinship. You are involved in Divine collaboration to shift realty to one that is preferred. The intention brackets or selects the frequency and points of contact, the index, the reality transformation. With your fingertips touch the indexed points in the field of your colleague. This is a measure. You might touch the body, if that is where the field points are. You will feel the contact. As you find the contact points, align in your connectedness, in your center. Take a deep breath, and drop into the wholeness, the All That Is. You are the stone dropping into the oceanic arms of All That Is. Move with the experience. Ask what she/he is experiencing. What is your experience?

The harvest of the Quimby's seeding has just begun.

The basic elements are:

- Be present relinquishing any need or agenda to fix.
- Connect through your kinship with the matrix of All That Is.

- Engage through morphic field with serving intention.
- Drop into your heart, releasing intention.
- Be present and observe the way of universal love.

Web sites to explore: *www.noeticbalancing.com*, *www.mystery-school.com*, *www.thetahealing.com*, *www.matrixenergetics.com*.

Introduction

As a teenager, I sat in my back yard, looking into the night sky, trying to see angels. Why not? In the religious environment in which I was raised, they seemed to be such an important part of God's conversation with us. Even in the San Fernando Valley, the stars were beautiful and I felt elevated. I think I made up a few angels. Even if part fantasy, my aspiration to touch these emissaries of God handed me a deep intention that loosened my consciousness from its material grip and allowed me to journey among the stars. It set an intention that pulled toward me the possibility of a direct transcendental encounter.

I was inspired by biblical stories. John, on a roof top in Patmos, saw the sky open, revealing multidimensional realities that led him to the Holy City. Paul spontaneously found himself traveling out of his body into another dimension, not knowing which heaven he was in. Jesus ascended into a cloud of light. No one in my church really understood these great events. They were events that happened to other people a long time ago, and we should be satisfied with a belief that gave us some hope of receiving relief from our guilt. Discovering that Holiness lived within us was not for the likes of us. No personal access. Officially, that is, since the Council of Nicea. The Cathars of Southern France knew better. Better spiritually, but they weren't much on political finesse. Like Saint Francis, their bodies were something to subdue.

My church could only talk about how bad we were and that somehow Jesus was able to die for our sins. I was grateful, of course, but it seemed to me that I was being told that because he did a good thing, I should feel bad; I really didn't deserve it. Perhaps he was showing us how to *die into rebirth* for our sins. That would make karma an opportunity for better things, a transformational opportunity. Sin means missing the mark, so we are here learning marksmanship. Somehow the dogma of the day made it our fault. Or, was it all a smoke screen that was inserted into church thought a long time ago, so that we would not test the possibilities of hearing the still small voice within? It is a voice that is our innate inward path to an ancient truth, the inward path that is our doorway to Heaven, the doorway that John walked through on the Isle of Patmos.

Just believe, they said. Jesus said that we would one day do what he had demonstrated and even greater things. I was definitely for that. Test all belief, was the word. It seemed to me that I was being invited to participate in a great mystery. For me that became a life-long exploration to discover the accessible, tangible and practical mysteries of life and Spirit.

The mystery seemed to continue to deepen just ahead of each answer that I discovered. When I questioned at church, I was given doctrine and a stern look, even severe admonishment. This was unsatisfying and, for me, mildly anti-scripture, and certainly patronizing. When I read the scripture, I felt invited to seek more deeply. I came to experience an eternal love that appeared to regard human life and purpose in a very different way than I was led to believe.

I made the Bible my technical manual. Thought, imagination, and feelings began to interplay through my experience. This was not delusional. When I would imagine myself walking in a garden with Jesus, my feelings shifted and it was as if I were actually transported there. Out of that experience, thoughts arose as images floating up from deep within my psyche. I would empty my mind and focus on a point of light and take a deep releasing breath. The images that arose informed me that a secret lived in my soul. My inner sky opened. The Patmos within me opened its doors. As the dogma fell away, Truth revealed itself as myself, as a Divine Self. The dogma became empty words that fell upon the earth like autumn leaves, while the living word sang eternal serenades within my heart. I had begun my career as a *spiritual scientist*.

I could have been born into any religious tradition and followed a similar path. It seems that every scripture has guides for living and keys for spiritual awakening. The guidelines direct attitudes and behaviors that promote a good life. These are preferred by people who want to be good and have no inclination, or lack the courage, to look more deeply. For those who want to know the truth and discover who they are, the keys are there in every scripture. Human nature also appears such that in each religious lineage there is a group of self appointed (claiming God's appointment) who mask the esoteric keys and promote their own version of truth in order to sustain their own agendas. Perhaps they are just doing their best, but this is the true dark side, and it is currently the case in most religions, some kinder than others. As a rule of thumb, anyone that professes to have God's authority for telling you what to do or think should be carefully evaluated, if not immediately dismissed. That being said, this writing could be easily aligned with any spiritual lineage; however, if you have the willingness to do that, you are likely able to use the information as is without the aid of a dogmatic back drop.

I began my quest in earnest a half century ago. That seems like a long time. During that time I found genuine spiritual guides who were able to do spiritual things rather than only talk about them and exhort unthinking, sometimes unloving, belief. I met many good people who practiced their faith and had a genuine close relationship with holiness. A few were actually way showers to higher realities. These encounters were my *road to Damascus,* and my *Isle of Patmos.*

As time passed, the main spiritual influences in my life came from the practice of Soul Transcendence, which is a form of Soul travel, my road to Damascus. Through initiation into the sound current, the audible component of the spiritual energy and the metaphysical understanding of consciousness as energy takes form as inner sound. I discovered that this sound was the "word of God." This inner experience of the "word" had a quality of limitless love and a call home. Ah, I thought, so it is we who made God dark, and gave over our will to the illusion of spiritual authorities, while, in truth, we spoke, at best, no more than our inspired opinion. We must ask, were we vigilant when our ministers spoke their inspired opinion and said it was the word of God? Were we vigilant when the inspired scribes of old, who, touched by the political winds of power, insisted that the words they wrote on blank paper were God's words, effectively turning away the angels that sang serenades within their hearts, inviting them home? Like Paul, I put aside the hypnotic dogmas of my childhood to embrace the living presence, face to face.

Noetic Balancing evolved from my first experience of spiritual healing. I discovered that the unknown void of the unconscious mind was actually full of all my unfinished business and surrounded my body as a force field of beliefs, most of which confined my perception to a small universe. These beliefs either resonated with Holiness, opening a conduit of spiritual energy and wisdom, or were dissonant, closing all awareness of spiritual connection. So, I thought, this is how we enshroud ourselves in shadow or open our hearts as radiant light. Each moment is a choice.

The basis for Noetic Balancing evolved out of the technique of aura balancing. Dr. Neva Dell Hunter, founder of Quimby Center, developed aura balancing from the healing work of Phineus Parkhurts Quimby and material gained through her inspirational work with John-Clark McDougall. The other member of this team was Ellavivian Power, who wrote the definitive book on balancing called the *Auric Mirror.* Quimby was an American Transcendentalist who developed a form of spiritual healing in the mid-1800's that he called the "Science of the Christ." I developed Noetic Field Balancing from my experience as a student at Quimby Center, thirty-five years of clinical experience, and academic work as founder and president of Southwestern College.

I met Dr. Hunter in 1966 through a mutual friend, Muriel Engle. Because I was experiencing a great deal of inner pressure, a lack of direction, and an inability to study, I had dropped my classes during my senior year at the University of California, Santa Barbara (UCSB). At the time of our meeting, Dr Hunter explained that aura balancing is a form of spiritual therapy in which the practitioner works directly with the energy fields surrounding and penetrating the physical body. The practitioner approaches the self as energy and directly engages the psychological trauma, analogous to the way a surgeon physically touches an organ. In response to emotional disturbance, mental anguish, and spiritual imbalance, we make judgments, which create blocks that reflect in the fields of energy that surround us. With the help of the Light (as she called it), the practitioner assists by finding these blocks and leading us into self-forgiveness. It sounded good to me. I agreed to a session. At the time, my exploration of consciousness-oriented psychologies and spiritual experiences helped me trust the process.

The impact was dramatic. I experienced energy sensations and feelings moving in and around my physical body, and a mysterious resolution of my inner conflicts. Afterward, I felt clear, centered, and ready to complete my senior year.

After graduation from UCSB, I headed for Dr. Hunter's school in New Mexico. I was excited about this profound demonstration of therapy. Conventional therapies had seemed lacking, and aura balancing represented to me the missing link that joined my experiences, spiritual training, and academic studies into one model. I needed to discover how it worked. To this day the mystery is larger than my discovery; however, I did expand upon the original technique based on my unfolding experience. From my perspective, the current practice encompasses a greater reality than how we were practicing aura balancing. I call the current form: *Noetic Balancing*.

At Quimby Center, I met Ellavivian Power and Stephen Broscoff who developed a body-centered approach. As an apprentice and colleague, I worked and lived with this team from 1968 until Dr. Hunter's death in 1978. After this time, my approach to balancing was influenced by my study and practice of "soul transcendence," with John-Roger Hinkin. John-Roger, founder of the Church of the Movement of Spiritual Inner Awareness (MSIA), adapted aura balancing to work with a spiritual consciousness that he called the "Mystical Traveler."

The greatest blessing is the deepening and softening of my heart and the wisdom that is conveyed to me with each person with whom I work. I am able to present myself to the Holy Spirit and to the service of souls in a way that promotes spiritual progression, health, happiness, well-being, and healing. I believe my role is to be a spiritual enabler, guide, or tutor. I am able to gently suggest and draw out the client's inherent wisdom. When all goes well, I am able to help them remember and touch the reality that they are originally and inherently divine. In a sense, I am an educator who can enhance the student's *soul-astic* achievement. When our souls touch, we awaken more to the immensity of spirit.

My studies have always followed the two tracks of spiritual and conventional wisdom. On the conventional side, I earned a BA and MA in Sociology, and an EdD in Education and Counseling. I became a licensed counselor. This background enabled me to found an accredited, spiritually based graduate school for counselors and art therapist.

From my perspective, Psychology is at the same crossroads as is religion. Just as religion confronts itself with its own dogmatism, hoping to find grace through its self-elevated view of its own righteousness, institutionalized psychology defends its arbitrary claim to exclusive wisdom, as it struggles to remain the "academy." Having said that, the religious and academic establishment is not made of one cloth. It is a consortium of individuals, some of whom find that a more integrative approach to achieving genuine health and well being is the effective response to the challenges of today.

I participate in an ever growing circle of colleagues. Most of us have never met. What we have in common is an interest in collaborative approaches to human health and well being. We are self selective. We reach out into the darkness with our light, knowing that the other is there. We quietly integrate empirical and heuristic approaches to the science of psychology with mysticism and quantum physics, forming a new technology and vocabulary of consciousness. We turn inward to find an awaiting covenant with eternity allowing truth to shape us rather than trying to shape truth with dogmatic agendas. Our response to fear is to embrace fearlessness and opportunity. We return to our spiritual roots: to first know our self and to seek the heaven within, knowing that the jihad is within us.

This writing contains the necessary wisdom and guidance to do Noetic Balancing. Information is always a risk because it can delude us into believing that we know. Information can also remind us, and awaken us to the wisdom that is in the ancient archives of our soul. We achieve the right use of this wisdom by taking one step at a time. With each step a change occurs within us that makes possible the next level of understanding. This process is best undertaking through the prudent use on inner and outer guidance.

Experience mediates the dance between information and truth. Wisdom is living energy. The ability to remind ourselves of our inner wisdom through the stimulation of written or spoken words is invaluable for anyone that is seeking a deeper understanding of life, especially with the intent of living better, with more grace and holiness. Words that come from the inspiration of our soul carry a living energy that transmits wisdom, invisibly communicating through our shared reality.

Currently, each school of psychology has its own province. For example: *Behaviorism* changes our behavior. *Psychodynamics* assists us to integrate and reorganize our healthy ego structure. *Humanism* processes our emotions and connects our actions with our feelings in a way that is congruent with our heart. *Archetypal* makes conscious our unconscious drives and facilitates actualization and fulfillment. *Transpersonal* connects us to our transcendental self, and awakens our awareness to universal themes and enlightenment. Viewing these various approaches as separate only perpetuates the perennial turf war of academic prestige and power, as it has for centuries. Taken together, however, they form a coherent model of the multidimensional human and its natural quest for health. Yet, we continue to divide up the human, perpetuating the universal dysfunction.

As an undergraduate, I began to see that fear was the glue of professional education and practice. Fear driven professionalism instills a subliminal adversarial tension into our enquiry and dialogue. Trust in ourselves and our inherent ability to know opens our ability to know directly from our experience. Thus, my heroes became the theorists and teachers who used first-hand phenomenology as their research methodology. Carl Jung, Fritze Perls, Carl Rogers, Abraham Maslow, and Rollo May were gripping examples from the psychological perspective, as were David Bohm and Edmund Husserl from the scientific perspectives. I found the work of spiritual travelers to be equally exciting, as represented by Hermes Trismesgistus, Pythagoras, Lao Tzu, Rumi, Gautama Buddha, Jesus Christ, Ralph Waldo Emerson, Phineus Parkhurst Quimby, and Rudolph Steiner. All of these individuals trusted who they were and used that center to discover truth.

Other forces were at play for me as well. On the dawn of the 60's, as a participant in a sensory deprivation experiment, I discovered that spiritual realities were directly observable. In the mid-'60's, as a participant in the civil rights movement, I discovered that character strength could be a force for social transformation. Meanwhile, Quantum Physics gave birth to the notion of the "observer effect"—that observation itself affects outcome. Gone was the illusion of certainty. I discovered that there is no "objective" science or objective God. I loved the way the '60's challenged my '50's reality. The social order appeared ready to deconstruct itself and to open to a new spirit of human potential. My academic goal thus became one of blending material and metaphysical wisdom into a unified curriculum for the purpose of individual well being and social change.

By founding Southwestern College, my colleagues and I were able to explore a core curriculum that integrated conventional and spiritual wisdom into an accredited academic program. The core curriculum focused on character first, then professional orientation. It was a "cleansing of the heart" first approach.

This was, to me, an antidote to the conventional "washing of the brain" method that appeared to inhabit much of my academic experience.

When we genuinely engage, each moment becomes a therapeutic experience that we share with each other and with life. Some people reading this book can move forward with what it teaches and have the consciousness to do very well. With my own students, I require that they do my wisdom school program first, and then study the balancing work. In our conventional consciousness, we are, to some extent, shut off from our multidimensional nature. Some of the dimensions are the repressed and neglected realms of our unconscious. On the other hand, there are also realms of heightened well being: states of consciousness that the ancients called *heaven, bliss, nirvana, enlightenment*. As our depth emerges, we encounter difficult psychic energies that must be resolved. An experienced mentor is invaluable when resolving our inner creations. The depth of our teachers reminds us of the depth within us. Always ask, does your teacher invite you into your depths, or onto the beach to build sand castles that will inevitably wash away in the changing tide?

This writing will open a doorway into a broader and deeper understanding of self healing, academic psychology, and counselor education, through which the force of spirit and soul can flow into our minds, open our hearts, and elevate our consciousness. If we are to discover the secrets of life, we need courage and trust in our capacity to know. Those secrets are available to us.

The idea that the ancients were enlightened is more than just a mythology. By ancient, I do not mean primitive. Primitives share with moderns the amnesia of the original soul. Ancient wisdom is indigenous and transcendental. Indigenous wisdom tells us where we are and remembers the *soul of the earth*, pulling access through her from the great heart of the universe. Transcendental wisdom opens a path inward, accessing the celestial vortex of light and sound that returns us *home*. When we know our true source and place, we have the key to transforming life on earth into grace.

Paradoxically, we are evolving and awakening through our trials and tribulations, to remember our intentional design. Myths point to prior high points in human evolution that have all but disappeared into the sands of time. With gentle intention, their meanings now re-awaken in the contours of our hearts. In our quantum reality, the past exists as a dimension of the present. When we are unconscious of this, the errors of the past continue to shape the present. When we are conscious of it, the ancient wisdom of the soul permeates our contemporary awareness, and we make life new.

This writing is an invitation to loosen your perception, allowing your mind to reach out to new thoughts and new intelligence and to ascend to new levels of your heart. Once that occurs, your reflection on the material will open internally to the wisdom of the soul. From that opening will come the knowledge of our complete nature and our role in eternity. Our clients, students, colleagues, and friends will be the beneficiaries.

As you explore this material, do so with a prayerful, respectful, accepting attitude. From my perspective, the material in this book is very accessible and practical, and ready to apply; however, I caution you to gain sufficient experience before you apply these techniques to others.

A well centered approach will provide you with a good understanding of the material, and will be useful on several levels of application: self help, intellectual curiosity, applying elements to your professional practice, or by participating in my program. If you are interested in learning my approach to balancing after reading this book, contact me at *rdw2110@aol.com*. For a course description go to my web site: *http://mystery-school.com*.

Spending time with me as a participant in the *noegenesis* and *practitioner* courses, as an integral part of your study of this material, would be a distinct advantage for you. For starters, the interaction with like minded colleagues sharing in-depth study is the best way to learn and to have valuable reflection for your internal process. My experience over the last forty years is invaluable. In that time, while deepening my relationship to this understanding, I have refined ways to guide and reflect to students the pieces in their foundation that need work, and to model the possibilities inherent in the transformational process. There is a degree of mastery that, when I teach, expresses as an acceleration of learning and personal transformation through the unified field of the classroom. Most of all, the quality of your alignment with higher consciousness and the refinement of your personal understanding are the essential keys to quality transformational work with others. In this arena, I am an expert tutor. I know how to draw out what you already know, to sort the ego's illusion and fantasy from truth, and to strengthen the soul's discernment. I understand that you may have an excellent understanding; however, in my experience, the higher you go the challenges within and in the field of your activity increase in subtlety and illusiveness. When mastering therapeutic transformation, we are also mastering how we create our reality.

This writing is an articulation of life's gift to me. Please make this reading, and your reflections, a gift to yourself. We are the invisible colleagues, illuminating shadow places in the collective heart of humanity. Once upon a time, we looked into the night sky, and we were welcomed by the stars.

Chapter One

STUDENT'S MIND

Student's Mind is the exercise of our perennial ability to learn, discover, and change. It is an expression of our identity as essence. In that sense it is *nous*, the first emanation of spirit into form. From the perspective of *Student's Mind* each therapeutic action is a journey into the unknown. Always proceed with anticipation and innocence. Be honored with the invitation to journey into the realms of evolving holiness that are actualizing through yourself, your client, and your friends.

The telling mind discovers nothing. *Student's Mind* aligns with the karmic flow of others tracking and aligning with the soul and its actualizing and transformational journey through this life. *Student's Mind* reads just as easily from the viewpoint of you as therapist, or teacher to yourself, on your journey of discovery and transformation of self. Ultimately our clients are a reminding mirror of what we have not yet resolved in ourselves. There is only One. So, assisted by the reflection of the client, we first forgive ourselves, each time reconciling with *nous*, the original blessing, life seen and lived through *eyes made of soul*.

Student of Self

We are first a student of ourselves, and through this sacred study, the mysteries of life unfold to us. In our natural way of discovery, we are spiritual scientist. Most of what we call knowledge, or wisdom, is, in reality, belief. One of our basic tenets is that scientific study can be objective. That is a belief. So, we believe we are objective and that what we are observing is objectively observed. We are experiencing our natural predisposition to behave as if the world, as we see it, is, in fact, how it really is. By deconstructing the so called facts, as they appear, truth reveals itself. We can begin with facts as they appear. We may even agree on what is factual. The fact that we agree makes it seem true, and it may not be truth. All life is formulated from a myriad of intentional currents that are actualizing life itself. In truth, we are constantly creating our reality through a process of negotiation that we call perception.

What is belief? Beliefs bind energy into the formation of precepts. Beliefs create the illusion that life is fixed, or static, when life is actually a continuous, ever-changing flow of experience. Once formed, beliefs block new information by determining that only information consistent with the belief can be received. Beliefs select the portion of reality that corresponds to its precepts. Does this mean that we must not have belief? Not at all. But, we do need to know what beliefs are and how they shape our perception. The behavior of creating and transforming beliefs adds substance to our soul. It is a gift of life.

The *Student's Mind* unfolds in the distinction of *acceptance* and *belief*. This is a tool that enables us to embrace new understanding without becoming negatively affected by false understanding. Simply stated, we accept everything and only believe that which works for us. By accepting, we do not block new information or understanding that may be coming our way. By not believing without appropriate testing, we do not buy into anything that is not true for us. Beliefs are the psychological building blocks of our perception. When we adopt a belief, it becomes part of our structure, thus affecting our perception and how we process energy. If a belief is contrary to our nature, you can imagine the problem: the way we experience reality is in opposition to our Divine nature. We live backwards.

Acceptance enables *Student's Mind* to flow with a current of unfolding understanding that is as continuous as breathing. You might say "I know what that means." When we respond in that way, we actually block our ability to learn spiritually. We would be better off saying "Hmmm. That's interesting," or, "I don't know. Please tell me more." The posture of knowing is often a protection. Not knowing is vulnerable and if we are not secure within ourselves, we will defend ourselves. We often fortify our self-esteem by posturing knowledge or expertise. Higher consciousness will not inflict new understanding upon us when we have signaled that we already know. By saying we know, we often miss the chance to really know. In this sense, *noegenesis* (apprehending new understanding directly from experience) is the power of now. Through the courage of being present, all life brings what we need to us.

We are truly a microcosm of the macrocosm. Our multidimensional nature reflects the form and processes upon which nature and the universe function. By embracing our mistakes, we can build a tested set of understandings about life. We have distorted and blocked our health in many ways. Knowing that is a cause for celebration, because those distortions become stepping stones to truth. The transformation of these blocks and distortions results in greater clarity and competency as a human being. We need the experience. Our access to higher consciousness is through our selves. We are not the Source, yet we connect to Source through its essence within us. We need perception that enables us to see and connect with our essence. The essential nature of *Student's Mind* is to discover, then test that discovery in order to reveal a yet deeper level of reality. Official knowledge, as we are accustomed, is death to the soul, or at least our ability to walk on this earth as a full incarnation of soul. We are made to live fully in this world, fully conscious of *nous*. When nous and soul shape our persona, we are living in the world, but we are not shaped by the world. We then create in life according to the likeness of our original blessing. *Nous*, then, is *student's mind*.

Perception

We need a mind that is receptive and active, rather than defensive or aggressive. As we practice *Student's Mind*, we devote a lot of time to developing our ability to sense, experience and direct *energy*, and learn the function of *symbols* in the deciphering of multidimensional meaning. We develop skills that enable us to track, deconstruct and reconstruct beliefs. To transmit the living energy of Source our beliefs must be congruent with our divine nature. In this process, we free ourselves and our self concepts from the fear based reality that preserves concept of self and the continuity of self based on the *status quo*. Through this process, we align our sense of self and continuity with Soul and our I Am (Divine) nature. We also learn how to center and use that centering as a nexus for aligning higher states of consciousness. By centering we open a conduit for living Source energy. When Source awakens in us consciously, it awakens in every cell of our body activating the *Source code* of our DNA, made dormant by external adaption.

To develop *Student's Mind*, we must embrace our eternity and create trust in our physical body. Our physical self needs to feel secure in the safety and leadership of a self that is not of this world, yet is enthusiastically living in this world. We are literally asking our molecular intelligence to reconfigure itself. Whereas our bodies are traditionally reassured by physical reality and a co-dependent psyche, we now ask them to form themselves based on physical reality and a Divine Blueprint. Through our enlightened bodies, we can reflect Heaven on Earth. We take care of ourselves so that we can take care of others.

From *Student's Mind*, perception is more than how we see reality. It is how we create reality. Perception selects how the universe responds to us. This is a key to healing and manifestation. In terms of Noetic Balancing, each element that is brought into greater balance subtly changes the individual's reality. Noetic (spiritual mind) lifts our thinking into a shared intelligence with creation itself. With Noetic Balancing, we are pursuing the innate goal of understanding the creation of self as the creation of reality. In order to do this, each session must be a new adventure. Your knowledge, experience and personal process is in the background. You approach the session with *Student's Mind*. This *mind* is more than an attitude. It is creation and the discovery of creation. As your soul overshadows your intellect your awareness moves into *Student's Mind*.

In the balancing practice, you are literally in an altered state in which you are perceiving through *eyes made of soul*. This has direct consequences on how reality unfolds in the balancing session. Your alignment is crucial to the level of work you are able to do. You are a spiritual scientist and your integrated body, mind and spirit is the research instrument. Through this level of perception, you are capable of understanding and working with the *spiritual physics* of your client.

Edmund Husserl

Edmund Husserl is the father of phenomenology. He mastered *Student's Mind*. He was interested in developing a science of philosophy. He discovered that by deconstructing the sedimented beliefs attached to a given phenomenon or thing, his perception became altered and he found himself in a state of transcendental awareness. He concluded that the structure of reality was the relationship of intentionality (archetype) and form (belief or physical structure).

He called the thing *noema* and the intentionality or essence *noesis*. These terms are extrapolations of *nous* (first emanation of spirit into form) and *noetic* (spiritual mind). Through the intentionality of mind, essence commands form. By deconstructing the sedimentation of the beliefs that are constellated to the form, essence, or truth, became evident. I find this remarkable. Through the simple trust in his human capacity to experience, Husserl developed a systematic approach to understanding directly through experience. This is how life teaches us. The act of apprehending new understanding directly from experience is called *noegenesis*. Husserl's protocol of discovery is the exercise of *Student's Mind*.

Husserl's protocol is "scientific" because the discovery occurs through the relationship (correlation) of indexed variables. Spiritual discovery takes two paths. One is transcendental, in which we seek a direct experience with Source. We engage our holiness through an experience of epiphany, revelation or enlightenment. We also seek an encounter of the sacred through the natural or phenomenal world.

The goal of Husserl's phenomenology was to understand. This is the behavior of *Student's Mind*. The protocols that he developed bear a close resemblance to yogic practices. The ancient mystery teaching looked at the "structure of experience" through sacred geometry, as the structure of reality.

noesis	noetic terminus	noema
("I" essence intentionality)	(experiential correlation)	(fact)

Husserl called the thing we want to understand, the thing as it appears, the "noema." The emergent understanding, he called the "noesis." The noesis is the experience of the "I" that intuits the essence that correlates with the fact of the noema. The structure of experience is the correlation of intentionality as essence and form. *Epoché* means to step back, to suspend our beliefs, or our usual ways of interpreting, or seeing. The steps to this process are called "phenomenological reduction." Reduction in this case is an extraction of essence, not a materialistic division of essence. It is a hermeneutic rule that guides the *Student Mind*. These steps give shape, focus, and direction to our investigation, interpretation, and learning.

Step 1. Attending to the Phenomenon or Experience as it Appears. This is the fact-stratum and constitutes a naive sense of given-ness. In other words, the object, or focus, is naively taken as it appears. We describe the phenomenon or experience, and suspend all tendencies to explain. All phenomena within the limits of what is given are equal. At this stage, we bracket the phenomenon and temporarily exclude all belief and knowledge. We become naive.

Step 2. Deconstruction. The given-ness is loosened so that what appears to be empirically ordered shows itself to be the result of a tacit context of beliefs. A shift occurs in this process that expands our awareness. Our perceptual topography expands from a fact-stratum to include an essence-stratum.

Step 3. Variations Are Explored. Through these variations, any intentional aim is intuited or becomes evident. This type of intuition is exact. What is intuited is self-evident because it is demonstrated in the perception. Once one sees a variation or intentionality, there is no doubt that one has seen it. We look for invariants in the structures or features within the variation of the phenomenon or experience. The fundamental structure of experience is transcendental.

Said another way, in phenomenological reduction, we:

1) Focus on the thing, expression, or belief that we want to understand or transform.
2) Bracket the phenomenon. Bracket means to exclude all else from attention except the phenomenon itself.

3) Deconstruct the localized belief, construct, or perceptual fixity regarding person, place, thing or belief. This engenders an altered state of consciousness that transports us to a transcendent experience.
4) In the transcendental or noetic mind, the correlating intention or understanding of the phenomenon directly presents itself as an experience of apprehending the *truth* or transformation.

Noetic Confluence

To engage the capacity of the soul as *inner teacher*, we must loosen the grip of the ego and it's socialized limiting belief systems. Through *Student's Mind*, we may begin by asking God, "Why?" In the analogy of boiling water, we have two answers. We can explain that the reason the water boils in a tea kettle is because the heat excites the molecules until the water boils. Or, we can say the water is boiling because we wanted a cup of tea. When we understand, the *why* is evident. Noetic learning bridges the implicate and explicate order of the subject matter in the experience of the student.

To the *Student's Mind* we live in a noetic reality. Discovery comes in the reflexive relationship of noesis and noema. Conventional learning occurs in perpetual dualism that sees as either/or, this/that, for/against, etc. It can never transcend itself. Dualistic approaches to discovery are adversarial and intellectual. Facts are correlated with facts as a basis of inference. *Student's Mind* correlates with *Living Love*. In this way, *Student's Mind* looks at life through *eyes made of soul*.

As in the ancient mystery teachings, Husserl's methods change the consciousness of the practitioner. It's like a Western yoga, a training for mystical understanding overlaid by the Western need for scientific rigor. He is not alone in this. As practitioners of *Student's Mind*, we are participating in the same wisdom. We are applying and responding to the same set of skills. The well being of the student and the adeptness of the practitioner are effects of the same grace.

F J Hanna points out, in *The Journal of Transpersonal Psychology*, that " . . . in Husserl's scheme, it would appear that such individual being's core boundaries are 'interpenetrated' forming a kind of transpersonal confluence in which there is a simultaneous, dialectical unity and separation of individual beings." (Hanna, p 185) Hanna elaborates on the similarity of the transcendent state described by Husserl as that of absolute being, recapitulating the steps of Patanjali's yoga: "concentration," "contemplation," and "realization."

Aspects of transcendental phenomenology are also reflected in Steiner's *Higher Worlds and Its Attainment*. He prescribes a similar training of will and focus as a way to develop the mind as an organ of spiritual perception.

Practicing Student's Mind harkens to the prophetic projections of Sri Aurobindo and Teilhard de Chardin. Aurabindo's perspective emerged from the Eastern yogas as the coming nexus of the mind of humanity with the supramental realm. Teilhard de Chardin called this realm the "nous-sphere" and believed that humanity's grasp of this realm is an emergent evolutionary potential.

Discipline

Alignment and balance are keys to *Student's Mind*. This is a discipline. Discipline makes us into disciples. In this sense *discipline* is as much a spiritual faculty as it is a practice. If we have greatly damaged our faculty of discipline, there will be a limit to our effectiveness as a noetic field therapist. Discipline unfolds from our natural will and ability to learn directly from Source. Centering affiliates us with Source. When we ground ourselves through our center into the center of the earth, we draw cosmic energy through the heart of the earth. When we reach up through our center into the highest spiritual dimension that we can engage, our hearts receive the Christ and the Holy Spirit, Allah, the Sugmad. Our witness and presence maintains this alignment. Witness is an active state in which we look through *soul eyes*, observing all manifestation in the world around us as a process of God. In mindfulness, we witness. We do not judge. We live in a constant deconstruction in which our sense of integrity emanates from living love.

Spiritual practice is essential. By engaging in a regular spiritual practice, you strengthen your anchor into the light and purify the miasmic distortion in the dimensions of your field. One way of purifying ourselves is through breathing practices. An easy way is to sequentially breathe the rainbow colors in through both ends of the *soul axis* into our hearts. On the exhale, we breath the colors into every cell of our bodies and then into the space around our bodies. Another example of purification breathing is to simply breathe in and hold your breath until you see a color and then exhale. Hold your breath at the end of the exhale until you see color and then inhale. You then repeat this cycle for awhile. These practices balance the *Student's Mind*.

Through the discipline of *Student's Mind*, we can access information from the level of the Father-Mother God. Father/Mother God is another name for the field of unconditional universal loving that we can access just beyond our own personal field. Vianna Stibal, in *Go Up and Work With God*, suggests that this place of access is sixty-seven feet or more above our heads. This distance refers to the geometry of how the dimensions interact with the physical body. When we are working with our own issues or health, or with a client, and we need more information, we can go up and engage the Father/

Mother God and ask to be shown what we need to know. It is simple. You go up and connect with the field of universal love and say "Father/Mother God, show me what I need to know." When you ask, you must also listen. Then test through *Student's Mind*.

Soul Eyes

In order to balance the *noetic field*, we must develop our ability to "see" energy patterns and perceive noetic reality. We must understand the structure and function of perception, and perception as a seeing organ of the soul and structure of the *Student's Mind*.

We construct meaning through our life experience. A major force in this process is our socialization. Much of perception is agreed upon through interaction with others. We project meaning onto the phenomenal world. To do *Noetic Field Balancing*, you learn to see past your projections into the essence of things and individuals. This practice requires that you forgive yourself each time you discover a limiting belief or viewpoint, or when you use your intellect to interpret experience.

In our three dimensional world, we are accustomed to seeing visible light refracting from surfaces. A light source reflects from a surface delineated shape and perspective to the rods and cones of our eyes, and then we take the sensation and translate it into meaning. What we see is rarely the pure stimulus. We actually see our own belief or memory. We equate seeing and perception. Perception is much, much more. What we actually "see" is the stimulus plus somatic and cognitive meaning. We develop our perceptual lens through experience. In this sense, we also see with our touch. Also, when we have an insight, we say that we see. This process is called intuition. All of these ways of seeing are expressions of perception. We could say, then, that meaning is the light source that illuminates our world.

In the implicate worlds of imagination, emotions, thought, archetypes and spirit, everything is a light source. Yet, meaning shapes that light to our consciousness. Then there is light that comes from beyond our meaning. We are in awe of this light. We are inspired, turn away because it is meaningless, or attenuate that light because we are afraid. *Student's Mind* sees through inspiration.

To see the aura, you must extend your awareness and allow your sensitivity to the subtle energies to emerge. We often comment on how "bright" or "radiant" someone appears. Something emanates from them that we describe in terms of light. We are beginning to see the aura. We also comment on our emotional state as being "dark," our mood as "blue," our anger as "red." We are seeing the aura. We are inwardly perceiving the energy of consciousness.

Just as we shape our communication through negotiation with others, we also shape our communication with invisible life. It is as if the spiritual realities meet us half way. The invisible intelligence of the universe is unconditional in its loving regard, so it will use whatever convention, image, symbol, or meaning we are capable of responding to. Once you engage these spiritual fields, you begin a transcendental dialogue through which you can be taught more refined modes of learning. In general the "teacher" is the higher consciousness of the noetic field. More specifically, the "teacher" can be the intelligence unfolding the phenomenon to you that you want to understand, or teachings that are embedded in your own spiritual structure. You may experience the dialogue of angels or beings of light, whose coherent life forms exist in the structure of noetic reality. *Student's Mind* communicates directly with the living intelligence of experience.

Through the application of *Student's Mind*, you develop your ability to work with the human energy fields. With practice, your perception and your ability to converse with higher consciousness improves. The mode of your communication becomes a language in itself. As such, it represents truth but it is not truth. In other words, these conventions reflect reality but are not reality. Clarity, discipline, and integrity are essential character attributes for developing the therapeutic communication required for implementing and facilitating the balance, alignment, and transformation of the human energy fields.

MAKING IT REAL

In my approach to psychology, therapy and teaching, the ability to be aware of *energy* is essential. For *Student's Mind* to function scientifically, it must be able to sense the impressions, pattern and changes in the energy field. Through energy awareness, *Student's Mind* can concretely and directly assess the subtle dimensions of consciousness.

Energy awareness becomes possible, by integrating our five senses with their multidimensional counterparts. Our bodies and the dynamic geometric etheric structures around it form an expanded sensory array. They are the forms that shape the movement of energy. These energies interact with the electro-biological energy of our physical bodies. These systems interface and have a relationship with etheric systems. As we align these systems, channels for the flow of spiritual energy open. No matter what level or dimension, we are always working with a combination of context and relationship.

The chakras are centers of power and consciousness that interface with their physical counterparts. They also interface with etheric counterparts that appear as geometric structures around the physical body. The relationship of these fields is subject to our mental, emotional and imaginal activity. The following protocol will enable us to explore our innate capacity to enhance and transform our consciousness.

As we explore the following practices, our perception will shift and reframe our consciousness. This shift in context is a form of reduction that changes our perception of the noetic relationship between noema (form) and noesis (essence). This is a shift from a sense of self aligned with form to a sense of self aligned with essence. When we organize our sense of self in our soul-center, *Student's Mind* accesses our supra-mental spiritual capacity to understand.

Eye Hand

Our bodies are bilaterally symmetric. This forms a polarity, and when engaged in relationship, it generates an energy field that can be used to charge up the aura, or bio-electric field.

1. Look at the palms of your hands as if you were holding a book at a distance of about a foot and a half from your face.
2. Allow your arms and hands to relax, while maintaining their relationship to your eyes.
3. After awhile, turn your hands so that the palms face each other.
4. You may begin to feel something between your hands. Move your hands back and forth. It may feel like a spongy ball. You may feel heat, or an attraction.
5. Push your hands together. As you rub your hands together you may hear a silky sound.

Looking at your hands builds energy. Exploring the sensations of the field between your hands activates your awareness. Rubbing your hands together charges you energy field. You can repeat this exercise several times for stronger results. In this exercise the body and your hands form the context. The posture orients your centers to form the relationship that generates the energy. In a sense, the reductive focus and postures unfold, or move, the energy, or chi, from the implicate noetic field into the magnetic field of your body and expand into the aura.

Rainbow

This exercise is the same as Eye Hand, with the addition of color visualization. The visualization creates a nexus with that color vibration in the universal field. We use the visualization of colors often in later exercises. Each color is a creative force in the universe, governed by a conscious being with which we can converse. (*See Chohans of the Color Rays,* by John-Roger.) The purpose of this exercise is to balance your energy and strengthen your understanding and awareness of energy. Do the entire sequence of the Eye Hand exercise with each color.

1. While looking at your hands with palms toward your face, visualize red and ask to be conscious and open to the awareness of the being (Chohan) of red. You can form a dialogue and ask how red functions in the universe. Red is an energizing, generative color. Then, turn your palms facing each other. Play with energy red. Observe the red vibration and see where it responds in and around your body. Rub your palms together and continue to the next color.
2. Visualize orange. Orange is energizing, supportive, and sustaining.
3. Visualize yellow. Yellow is mental energy and calms the mind.
4. Visualize green. Green is healing.
5. Visualize sky blue. Blue is the energy of Chi and elevates the consciousness.
6. Indigo. Indigo sensitizes the psychic force-field.
7. Purple. Purple energizes our soul relationship, and transcendental awareness.
8. Silver. Silver grounds us and connects us to the cosmic flow of energy through the earth, and transcendentally to Source.
9. Gold. Gold connects us to the source of love and power.
10. Turquoise (blue-green). Turquoise connects us to the mediating power of source.
11. White. White connects us to pure spirit and universal wisdom.

Ra Hu

As corollary of the Rainbow exercise, I sometimes introduce the Ra and Hu chant as a means of activating and teaching the power of sound and energy.

1. While doing the Rainbow Hand Eye exercise, chant "Ra" three times while visualizing orange. "Raaaaaaaaaa . . . ." This will build energy and introduce you to the effects of Ra.
2. While doing the Rainbow Hand Eye exercise chant "Hu" three times, while visualizing purple. "Huuuuuuuuuu . . . ." This will build transcendental energy and introduce you to the effects of Hu.

Circle Energy

This is similar to the previous exercises except that it is done with a group. The purpose is to explore the power of the group as a conduit and generator of energy.

1. Form a circle with your group, holding your left hand palm up and parallel to the floor at your sides. Hold your right hand over the left hand of the person next to you. Hands are not touching. (This can be done with only two people by standing facing each other with hands in front of you at about waist level with your left hand turned palm up and your right hand palm down over your partner's left hand.)
2. At an even pace, the group visualizes each color, with an optional chanting of "Ra" at orange and "Hu" at purple.

Pushing Space

The universe meets us at our focus and responds to us with that which we pay attention to. In this exercise, we will explore the nature of energy, substance, and space. This exercise is for two or more people.

1. Sitting opposite one another, notice the air between you and how we take for granted that there is nothing in this space. Face your hands toward each other, moving them back and forth, noticing the movement through space.
2. Consider that when we are dreaming, reality is solid to our dream body. Attune to the reality that the air around you is solid. Move your hands toward each other. Notice subtle changes. Perhaps the shift is not so subtle.
3. Repeat the exercise with another person, one being passive and the other active. You can also do this as a group. One group pushes space and the other experiences the effect of that.

In Chi-gung, we attune our consciousness to the blue space around us, collecting chi through our movements. Also, consider that thought impacts the space around us. Other people's thoughts impact you as your thoughts may impact others, especially if you place emotional force or intent with the thought. What is good thought ecology for the space around us? Focusing with greater subtlety, we discover that "heaven is at hand."

Nexus

Basic to our inner awakening and perceptual acuity is our ability to activate our center, calling forward our holiness, and aligning with higher consciousness. Each of the following steps adds to the previous one. It is an additive sequence.

1. See your body in the center of a sphere of light. This is your space. Call your holiness forward to fill your space.
2. Place your attention in the center of your head. This is a reductive focus in which you set aside all expectation and thoughts. Hold your attention for at least three breaths.
3. Place your attention high above the top of your head, and hold it there for three breaths, feeling your relationship to higher consciousness.
4. Place your attention in your heart for three breaths.
5. Look up at the star or point of light that is at the top of your sphere, extend your focus to that point and engage the energy that is there. Invite universal holiness to fill your space. (An option is to journey through the star and after awhile bring the universal holiness into your space.)
6. Relax and sustain your awareness, moving with any changes.

Chapter Two

SELF AS NOETIC FIELD

The traditional name for the human energy field is the *aura*. The *aura* appears to exist within a larger array of forces and geometries, which I call the *noetic field*. The *noetic field* is a broad concept that embraces the deeper dimension of spiritual essence and mastery implied by the understanding of self as energy and holiness. Rupert Sheldrik calls the noetic dimension the *morphogenetic field*. *Morphogenetic* means form making. This is the same inferred energy matrix that David Bohm, in terms of quantum physics, calls the *implicate order*.

Our "space" is our self as energy, holding and containing our embodied self. Noetic derives from *nous,* which is the first emanation of spirit from the formless to the form. It is the a-priori intentionality of which all creation unfolds, moves, and has its being. The term noetic refers to the fabric of consciousness, containing essence and form. To see life noetically is to see through *eyes made of soul.*

The aura, or energy field, surrounds and penetrates the physical body. As a more encompassing concept, the noetic field surrounds and interpenetrates this auric energy field, embracing our multi dimensionality from ego to Source. Historically, artists depict halos around the heads of individuals to denote spirituality. Biblically, writers refer to the "raiment" or "countenance of light" in an attempt to describe the field of spiritual energy around angels, men, and women. We use common-sense terms such as "blue mood," "red with anger," "green with envy," "full of energy," "radiant beauty," and "vibrant personality." Such terms are similar to how individuals with spiritual sight describe the energy field. It is common sense that we all have an unconscious awareness of our multidimensional connection to life.

Quantum physics describes the universe as energy. Energy and matter are interchangeable. Psychology, Eastern Yoga therapy, and complementary medicine have terms for life as energy. Some of the more well-known are "prana" (yoga), "chi" (acupuncture and chi-gung), "libido" (Western psychology), "orgon" (Reichian bioenergetics), "Holy Spirit" (Christianity), and "light" (universal spirituality).

Our minds are accustomed to the seemingly concrete terms for energy and energy fields, such as those caused by magnetism and electricity. The truth is, we understand electricity and magnetism in operational terms; that is, by our description of its effect. (i.e., electricity lights the bulb, or spinning the conducting wire around a magnet produces a current.) We can effectively proceed and predict outcomes within limited parameters of what we believe the reality to be. The heart of why, or how, they work is mysterious. For now, I will settle for operational constructs. This means, we can use the term energy, given that we are clear about the referential context and set of relationships. When I use the term energy, I strive to provide a sufficient reference point from which our intelligence can proceed. My use of energy enables me to predict results: to "light the bulb," or to "make current" to illuminate consciousness, or access the Holy Spirit.

The reality of self as a conscious energy field gives us a way to approach life itself as generative and therapeutic. An understanding of these field dynamics enables us to apply the mystery of transformation. This energy, though nonphysical, appears through a gradation of attributes specific to the dimension or realm one is accessing. We have instruments that can detect some aspects of these subtle realities; however, our individual physical, psychic and spiritual functions, at present, make the best instruments. Equally helpful is our capacity to metaphorically extrapolate the models of physics. Though it is clear that the energy of physics is different from that of metaphysics, there is value in the symbolic connection of the two. However, from the perspective of quantum physics, the difference in the two energies is less clear. Whatever the case the concept of "energy" helps us articulate our noetic experiences. Just as the atom is theoretically inferred based on its effects, we can infer the soul based on its mental, emotional, and physical effects. Though our technology has not yet given us vision into the atom, with spiritual sight we can see into the world of the soul. Through the *eyes of soul*, we can look into the universe of the atom and know where to direct our technology and how to interpret the information we gather. As we remember our ability to sense and see into subtle realities, we find that we are also able to interpret changes in this energy field. Our nervous system is linked to the noetic field. I suspect that at some point, we will discover that the energy of physics and metaphysics is the same, or, at least, is an effect of the same source.

In conventional therapy, we begin with the issue, explore its structure, and infer the blockage in the intentional flow of energy. When we approach therapy through the *noetic field*, we begin with the blockage of energy in the field itself as it exists around the physical body. Once the block is discerned and attuned to, we explore the related belief structure that holds the energy in its traumatized, limiting or dysfunctional form. Blocks are beliefs that impede or distort our perception and ability to actualize our lives. Blocks are choices that diminish our sense of self or separate us from our inherent goodness. Blocks stay in force because we believe in them.

Therapy through the *noetic field* is an approach that uses the spiritual alignment of one person to balance the personal energy field of another. In the balancing process, we assist another person to change, re-frame, or forgive themselves for the blocking beliefs or judgments. We link with the field of *living love* and *intelligence* that forms the background movement of the therapeutic relationship. As Apostle Paul said, "Let the mind be in us that is in Jesus." We are using our spiritual mind to focus and cooperate with the spiritual intelligence that is implicit throughout the material, psychological, and spiritual realms. In the practice of *Noetic Balancing*, therapy proceeds by focusing on energy first and image second. We reference our therapeutic attunement first on the energy field, followed by attention to the body and psychological structures. Our therapeutic focus forms a conduit for the flow of spiritual energy (such as chi, dharma, or the Holy Spirit). This flow of energy helps release the blocks, and balances the noetic field. When the distortions are gone, the field is once again fluid and smooth. As the field is re-energized, it resumes its natural function of nourishing the body, protecting the psyche, integrating the body, mind, and soul, and maintaining a resonance with the noetic field.

Mystery of the Cross

In the emerging course of this writing, the term noetic arises out of the synthesis of ancient wisdom and modern psychology. The *noetic field*, including what the ancients call the aura, is a dynamic system of contexts and relationships. The refinement of our psychological construction is a key to the balance and alignment of these systems.

The next consideration is that of energy. The cross is an ancient symbol for the interaction between the vertical access to the spiritual dimension and the horizontal actualization of life in this three dimensional world. This world is our experience of resolving the cause and effect of our soul's journey. It is through the interaction of the "cross" that we balance our psyche through application of *Noetic Balancing*. This is what I am calling the *mystery of the cross*. So in a biblical sense, we "resurrect" the Christ within us through the transformation of our "sacrifice" on the cross of life.

Basically the vertical element of the cross symbolizes the central access of energy that links "heaven" and "earth," or, in physics, the implicate and explicate order. It represents the energy that we source from spirit, or Holy Spirit, the pure energy that unfolds from the "nothingness." It is the energy that moved the first creation into form, the *nous*, the voice, or wind of spirit. It is also the return, the call to truth, essence, and return to Source, or home. It is the holiness that operates through an agreement, respect, honoring, unconditional love, and reverence for all life. It is the vertical axis of our center, as the flow of *living light* through us between heaven and earth.

The horizontal bar of the cross symbolizes the "magnetic energy," the energy of life from within the structure of creation. As "invisible" spiritual energy unfolds into form, the magnetic energy provides the conduit. Structures take shape according to codes that inform the energy field, thus the term *morphogenetic*. Similar forms attract each other. For example, we are attracted to places we like, as magnets attract iron. We might say that when we free ourselves from limitation through transformation or inspiration, we feel on fire. In an analogous way, fire is freeing the sun energy that was stored in the burning wood. From burning coal or wood to accessing the archetypes of personal power, patriotism or religious zealotry, what I am calling magnetic energy can be accessed regardless of the quality of our consciousness, or good or evil intent. We can use it freely based on choice, whether in adversity, domination or coercion, or protection, safety, or health. It also represents the actualizing vector of soul-fulfillment. The horizontal movement of the soul is the actualization of our life-span agendas. It is the essence/form relationship the structures experience.

The cross symbolizes that our center and balance in life is the equality of the horizontal and vertical actions. In the spiritual worlds, we are spirit. In this world, we are spirit and matter. Psychological stress, and imbalance in the energy field, reflects a distorted or imbalanced cross. When the aura is balanced, we become centered and radiant.

When I speak of the *noetic field*, the implication is that its energy is also a commingling of intelligence and love. The mystery of this love and intelligence begins in our initial awareness of polarities and contrast, and evolves into the inclusion of tertiary associations. Any duality, dichotomy, polarity has a third element of unity. The evolution of our life and intelligence progresses through contrast and shifts into noetic understanding as we experience this third pole of reality. The duality is the magnetic axis of the cross and the trinity is the vertical, or spiritual axis. The magnetic provides the visibility of the spiritually invisible. The cross also symbolizes the purposefulness of our life expression. The cross symbolizes the *intelligence* evolving through *living loving*.

Noetic Levels

The following figure is a beginning representation of the noetic field's dynamic structure. The diagram shows the physical body and its relationship to the chakras, or energy centers. Each center correlates with specific psychological functions: *Root* is energy and support; *Sacral* is creativity and sexuality; *Solar Plexus* is power, security and belonging; *Heart* is love, courage and relationship; *Throat* is communication and symbolic awareness; *Brow* is seeing; *Crown* is perception and transpersonal awareness. I added a center at the feet to represent the chakra of *place*. I did this because of the dynamic of belonging and its powerful effect on the entire field. Also, I added a transcendent chakra. This chakra is our nexus with spirit, a holy place where we "worship spirit in spirit." For now, we can call this the *I Am* chakra. It also allows us to operate in the dynamics of self that are independent of the time-space continuum of our everyday life. Of course, there are more dimensions. These are the primary dimensions that directly relate to the balancing action of noetic *therapy*.

The two interlaced triangles are the integration of above and below. They are the two-dimensional image for the star-tetrahedron, which, in turn, is the sacred geometry of our light-body. *Spiritual Physics* is the application of sacred geometry, and perhaps Quantum Physics as well. Our multidimensional nature expresses as geometry. When we organize our psychology according to outer indices, the light-body slows and dims, and our DNA re-sequences itself to density. When we organize our psychology according to our light-body, our DNA sequences to its inherent, natural rhythm of light. The curved lines reflect the universal flow of magnetic and spiritual *light* and *sound* as it "breathes" through the geometric, vertical, mental, emotional, imaginal, and physical expression. This can also be depicted as a column of light through the vertical axis of the body and personal space. Subjectively, we identify the phenomenon of the vertical axis phenomenon as "our center." The purpose of it all is to provide experience to our souls. The light-body serves as circulatory system between the central axis as a conduit of spirit and center, the morphogenetic field that holds the form creating information of our incarnation, and our physical body.

Each level of consciousness develops from a root pattern of archetypes. These root patterns act like a mirror for the denser energy. Our health is based on how truly our lives resonate with these archetypal genetics. Healing is a matter of bringing imbalances into a healthy resonance with the root pattern, or genetic archetype. The needed pattern could be provided by a substance, ritual, or a change in understanding. Spirit, being the essence of all root patterns, is able to balance any pattern, provided it does not violate the free choice and path of the individual creator, or the integrity of the primary pattern of the whole.

"Chakra," a Sanskrit word meaning "wheel," is a central organizing principle of yoga psychology. The function of each chakra matches the levels of meaning in Maslow's hierarchy of needs, from a Western psychological approach. Huna is an indigenous approach to the same realities, developed by the ancient Hawaiians and continued by native and nonnative Kahuna practitioners. The psychosynthesis model was developed by Assagioli from his study of esoteric wisdom and experience as a psychotherapist. By overlaying the map of depth psychology onto the human energy fields and using the physical body as our point of reference, we can visually and imaginally explore the psycho-spiritual structures as relationships of energy. The preceding diagram presents Maslow's hierarchy of needs and the chakras on the vertical axis of the body. The levels of psychological functioning extend in contours from the body. Locally, the energy field is limited to our own space. Internally, each center is structurally vast.

The psychological functions are interactive levels. These levels are: *physical, etheric, imaginal, emotional, mental, archetypal,* and *spiritual.* We will explore these levels as structural dynamics that influence the flow of energy (or consciousness) through and around the physical body. Within these levels is a realm of consciousness that I call *soul-space.*

Soul-space is a refuge within us, ground of being, and Source to spirit. For most, awareness of this space begins as myth. It seems ephemeral. Conceptually, we may believe that we are inherently spiritual. Our soul-space grows as we reflect on our essence as spiritual; develop and observer relationship to our issues, traumas, and habits; meditate and pray more often; and forgive ourselves more readily. As we transform our experience and awaken spiritually, our soul-space grows. At some point, we realize we are *soul* living as the presence of peace, joy, love, grace, wisdom, and power. Solving our problems begins to seem less important than developing a soul relationship to our problems. We no longer define ourselves in terms of external viewpoints. Shame or blame may persist to a degree but it no longer forms any aspect of who we are. Our identity is in the realm of soul while our life in the world continues to interface through the province of the ego. Whereas ego was once given ascendancy, it is now demoted to middle management.

The etheric body is sometimes referred to as the "etheric double" because it is a template or archetype for the physical body. It appears as an energy matrix.

From one perspective, this system is described in chi-gung as the meridians of the body that transmit chi to the organs. The flow of chi is the flow of life force that maintains the health of the body. Eventually these meridians merge with the axial tonal lines that, as we develop, form a nexus with the universal flow of cosmic energy. The balance and alignment of the aura affects the functioning of the meridians. The chakras are a complementary structure to the meridians. Whereas the meridians interact with the organs of the body, the chakras interact with the endocrine system and nerve plexus. For all practical purposes, the etheric level of the aura is a subtle complement to the physical body.

Physical. Penetrates the physical and etheric bodies and reflects the state of the energy fields. When this level has a smooth, strong flow of energy, the body can accommodate enhanced forces deeper in the psyche. This level reflects physical trauma, cell memory, physical health, and somatogenic beliefs and emotions.

Etheric Double. A subtle counterpart of the physical body (not shown) that functions as an archetypal pattern or blueprint for the physical body. The meridians and chakras appear in this formation.

Imaginal. I depicted the imaginal level as a five pointed star because of the way it functions in the field. It is a function of imagination, thus it is a tool that we use to select frequencies of energy, connect to reality fields through symbols, and create environments. It is the medium through which we create and transform our circumstances; sometimes called the "astral" level. We develop this level as a function of inner and outer perception, intention and creativity. It is also highly susceptible to delusion.

Excessive fantasy, created out of recreational drug use, or an intention to escape or avoid, can create forms in the aura that are disconnected from the authentic processes of creativity. As a consequence, inner realities are created that are disconnected from the ability to complete, fulfill, or enhance the soul's purposes. In other words, these self created forms effectively help us avoid life and the challenges and rewards that our soul is destined to fulfill.

The imaginal level develops into a highly integrative and creative ability, serving shamanistic, transcendental, and actualizing purposes. Much of art therapy works through the power of this level. In noetic therapy, we balance this level as part of the physical and emotional balancing. Drugs promote imaginal fantasy, delusional thinking, emotional confusion, and congest the physical level from.

Keep in mind that the levels of the aura penetrate and ride across each other. For therapeutic purposes, we learn to focus our attention on one level at a time. This provides a type of distinction due to our focus on one level. To work with each respective level, we focus on that level. By doing so, our consciousness excludes everything else that is not our focus.

Delusions and obsessions are generated through and reflected in this level. On the other hand, intention, positive self-image, image dialogue, construction and integration through imagery (as in psychosynthesis), visual learning, visualization and healing, manifestation, and success are all generated and reflected by this level. Used dissociatively, the imaginal level can be devastating. Used integratively, it is a powerful force for connecting, integrating, and aligning all the levels.

Emotional. Carries the artifacts of our feelings and emotional reactions and actions. Our emotions give life to our beliefs and judgments and the impetus to pursue our vision. For this reason, this level reflects an aspect of our dharma or *causal body*. "Causal" is translated from Eastern systems as the karmic-dharmic expression of our soul. It is the force that determines and sets the causation into our lives, which our soul subscribes to fulfill.

From that perspective, when we are neutral, we might assume we are not creating karma (actions that must be completed or reconciled.) We may also not be creating at all. A more effective way to keep this level healthy, vital, balanced, and karma-free is to act through powerful, universally oriented, nonmanipulative, and unconditional loving. The destiny aspect of our causal nature is reflected through the archetypal level.

This level is the Source of our drive for power and dominance. It powers our adversarial and competitive nature. It also is the Source of passion, the total embracing, and the loving heart that heals and forgives. It reflects our warmth, our devotion, and what we care about. It is also the peacemaker. Our emotional level registers our fulfillment and longs for peace.

Mental. Reflects our beliefs, concepts, and attitudes. Though feelings and emotions are often keys to beliefs, our mental activity decides what we will build as our internal structure and how we will project ourselves into life. Through our mentality, we construct our relationship to our destiny, karma, and inner life. Balancing the mental aura is most similar to conventional depth and ego psychotherapy. Through our instinct for preservation, we take our beliefs as truth, as permanent, as the pillars of our existence. As a spiritual activity, beliefs are a practice of simulated realities serving transitory purposes. Some beliefs are couched in duality and cause us to resist and battle with ourselves. All beliefs ultimately serve as stepping stones to our enlightenment. Forgiveness is a key force in mental balancing: receiving forgiveness, forgiving others, and, most importantly, forgiving ourselves.

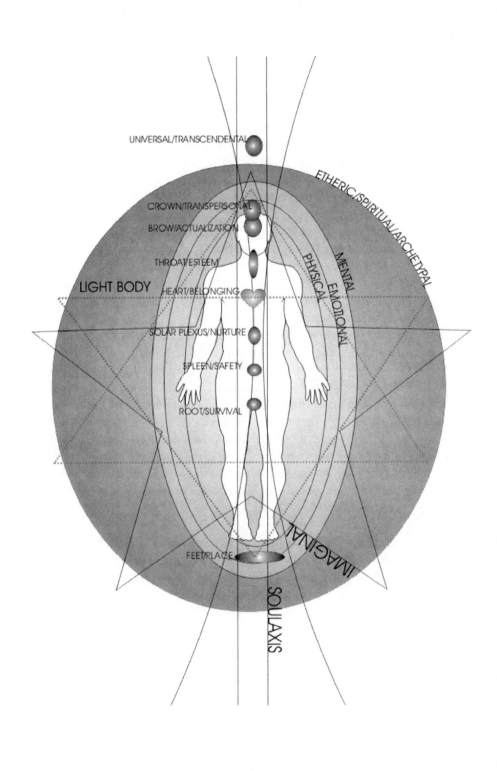

The mind is the constructor, the builder. This level reflects our associative activity through which we internalize and develop our integrative learning and personality. It is also dissociative and reflects the constraints that divide us from and within ourselves, and from each other. We shape our reality with our minds. Mental health or illness is reflected in this level. The capacity of the mind ranges from instinctive-intellectual to intuitive-reflective thinking. At the highest level, the spiritual intellect of cosmic consciousness or enlightenment merges the personal intellect with the superconscious, divine mind.

A main premise of this writing is that our minds are ripe for evolution, for a morphogenetic transformation. As we shift from ego to spiritual-mind (noetic), we activate our genetic structure and reach into a deeper level of our human potential.

Archetypal. Contains the map of our destiny, sometimes called the "etheric level" because it is the template or matrix for existence as an extension of our soul. Barbara Brennan calls this level "ketheric." I have heard it described as a "cosmic mirror" on which our life plan is imprinted. The soul sits on the other side, "looking" at life as through a two-way mirror, living in "paradise," radiating into life through the patterns of destiny. From the ego's perspective, we only see the reflected light of the soul and the shadows of our destiny. The scenario symbolically portrayed on this mirror reflects into our mental, emotional, and physical lives as our destiny. It is much like a spiritual genetic code. When our lives reflect given states of consciousness, or the accomplishment of certain lessons, adjustment is then permitted in the archetypal field. The archetypal level changes when we put in our time, pass the test, or awaken to the soul.

When reflected outside of us, we see the archetypes as the pantheon of gods. When internalized, these archetypes are the angels of destiny, the gods that dwell within us. It is the structure of intentionality.

Each culture has its mythology. Archetypal forces tend to dominate the personality until one's experience and development secures one in a sense of soul. When this happens, inner wars subside and cooperation between the internal and transcendental archetypes occurs. As this transformation occurs inwardly, peace is possible in social, economic, and political manifestation.

Archetypes form the themes of our lives individually and collectively. Events symbolically reflect inner processes. The symbolic and archetypal formation reflects themes that portray destiny. As life-long learning, our destiny is synonymous with our soul's curriculum. We came into life with an internal, archetypal lesson plan. At the archetypal level, we choreograph the mind, emotions, imagination and physical actions. We transform the archetypes that contain and drive our expression. When we become conscious of ourselves as soul-selves, we transcend and master these powerful forces. As our awareness of the soul-self increases, we become a conscious executive capable of coordinating and experiencing reality beyond these archetypes, while living through them.

The archetypal level is our unconscious. There is collaboration in human activity through the collective unconsciousness. As individuals awaken to the inner realms, beyond the collective and archetypal ceilings, the collective is transformed. The phrase, "If I can be lifted up, I will draw others to me," is more than a dusty Biblical admonition. It is a strategy for transformation. The archetypal level appears inwardly as the ultimate consciousness. It is the highest state we can reach through our ego while remaining egoistic in our approach to life. Each religion has its way of explaining this. As the self-as-ego diminishes and the self-as-soul is enhanced, we increasingly experience ourselves as innately one with everything and everyone.

In the Native American culture, the medicine wheel is an example of the archetypal level. The medicine wheel forms a symbolic geography that enables the individuals to orient themselves in the cosmic scheme. The alignment of a connection to place, spiritual and physical, is an essential aspect of our ability to balance our energy, awaken to ourselves, and orient ourselves to life. The four directions give us place while the animal spirits give us our power and kinship with our transcendental origins.

Our noetic capacity slumbers within the unconscious as an archetypal form, a soul genetic potential, awaiting our conscious awakening. As the noetic mind awakens, we begin to see into our unconscious without the need to reflect its content symbolically and our dreams gain greater lucidity.

Spiritual. In the diagram, the spiritual and archetypal is depicted as an encompassing orb simply because the spiritual permeates everything, while the "membrane" with the archetypal and the spiritual functions as a mirror or a nexus, depending on the awareness of the individual. The spiritual reflects and responds to the balance and alignment of all the levels. In this level, the balancing energy acts as wholeness. It moves through the chakras and levels as a process of breathing.

Each of the other levels provides a conduit for spiritual energy. As the noetic field balances, aligns, and strengthens, the spiritual level becomes more evident. It reflects our transcendent nature into our psychological, social, and physical realities.

The spiritual level is hard to articulate except through shared experiences or stories that reflect actual experiences of spiritual realities. For that reason, most religions rely on dogma or a set of beliefs or principles to anchor their faith. Though often overburdened with dogma, most religions practiced from a pure intent and righteous heart, yielding genuine spiritual experience. Within all faiths there is an inner group that moves beyond the dogma into a living relationship with the transcendent and present Holiness. Our personal sense of spirit develops in a central way in our soul-space where we live as spirit and express and differentiate ourselves through the various levels.

The spiritual level of the aura becomes more apparent as we organize our personality and psychospiritual structure with soul as the conscious center of the way we perceive, think, feel, imagine, and act physically. The degree of our centering in ego or in soul reflects into the overall ambiance of the energy fields. Life-long learning is a personal *soul-journ*ey and an actualization of universal love. Soul-space is where we are aware and embody self as soul. We experience soul as the individual awareness of universal love.

What imbalances the noetic field?

Noetic Balancing is powerful and direct. The inner dimensions of our psyche appear around our physical body as layers of beliefs, emotions, and archetypal forms. Our issues and concerns appear as blocks and distortions in the energy patterns of this field. The blocks and distortions are caused by physical and emotional trauma, self judgment and limiting beliefs, or from external psychic pressures from individuals, groups or institutional belief systems. The blocks and distortions affect the containment and movement of energy within our consciousness, and may result in psychological problems or physical disease. The indiscriminate use of recreational drugs or alcohol can severely damage the noetic field.

Blocks can be an attempt to protect. As such, they become integrated into the sustaining structure of our personality. As we create meaning in response to trauma, we adapt to that meaning as if it were normal. Thus, the trauma, and the resulting meaning that we construct, become normalized. We adapt to the level of our injury, and then believe that is who we are. Consequently, as we become more centered through balancing, our sense of self shifts from ego to soul.

While our ego adapts to trauma, our soul continues to pursue transformation. In the deepest sense, our field is out of balance as one phase in a process caused by our drive to awaken spiritually and transform the quality of our lives and our experience. In a more conventional sense, any concern, trauma, or issue that brings us to counseling, or requires therapy, reflects in our field as an imbalance.

Through prayer and focus, an altered state of consciousness unfolds, enabling the practitioner to engage the blocks and distortions directly in the energy field. Through this spiritual rapport, the practitioner is able to assist us to transform and balance our consciousness. Transformation occurs through an alliance of intervening spiritual energies, unfolding soul energies, and our own self forgiveness. With practice, we can also be our own practitioner; however, the intersubjectivity of self reflection can make resolution illusive. On the other hand, life has a way of reflecting to us through experience and pointing precisely to that which we need to see.

Why Balance?

When our field is out of balance, so is our perception of and connection with life. Because imbalance and weakness appear in the field before it manifests in the physical body, balancing can be a preventive physical therapy, as well as therapy for the transformation of emotional and mental issues. By understanding the noetic field and directly engaging its distortions, we can transform the blocked energy created by trauma, choice, socialization, and daily challenges.

These sessions provide a powerful support, strengthening our alignment, center, clarity, and well being. It is an effective complement to therapy and healing, and promotes our spiritual progress. The effects of therapeutic balancing are often subtle, and at other times, very dramatic. The results of the session can range from deep relaxation to perceptual clarity, greater spiritual alignment, or enlightenment. When the field is balanced, it is fluid, smooth, and energized, resuming its natural function of nourishing the body, protecting the psyche, and integrating the body, mind, soul, and spirit. We may experience an expansive sense of well-being, greater enthusiasm, heart-felt presence, ease in daily living, more joy, or peace. More importantly, Noetic Balancing strengthens our connection and awareness of the spiritual centrality of our nature: our self as energy and Holiness. To realize this is to know the true nature of reality.

Chapter Three

FABRIC OF SELF

The true teaching occurs in the invisible fabric that is woven through our rapport with others, with environment and with transcendence. In this way, our *witness* reciprocally clarifies the intentional force of our soul-truth. In this way, the multidimensional energy can more easily unfold into our present conscious awareness, joining us, awakening in us, lifting, teaching, transforming. The *fabric of self* is woven through the co-creative intimacy of life. As we become increasingly aware and connected with life, we choose consciously to harmonize that fabric with the universe and our origins. This choice is our destiny.

Through the Looking Glass

I love this metaphor. When we look in a mirror, we see an image of our physical self that appears deceptively accurate. We unconsciously interact with this image, as if it is just fine. Our first clue that perhaps things are not as they seem comes when we discover that the image is reversed from left to right. A camera lens reverses the image from top to bottom. Once we know this simple rule of perception, our way of looking at reflected images changes. The reality of reflective light is that this three dimensional physical reality is the one in which we play out the drama of our discovery and accomplishment, until we see beyond the "looking glass." When we meditate on our image in the mirror, the image of our face changes, even disappears. Something occurs in our eyes that fatigues the receptors in a way that the concrete image doesn't hold and we see into the subjective dimension of the image.

I love to teach. One of the main reasons is that each session is a new revelation. Recently, a student raised a concern. She discovered that she had based her value on her relationship to her husband and children, and that career had always been a secondary consideration. She saw herself as the reflection given her by her family. Forgiving herself for the belief that she had to be whom her family wanted her to be in order to have value was very powerful for her. She realized that the reason she embraced that life for so long was because that was the way she learned to know herself, that was how she learned to be "herself."

Once she forgave herself and let go that viewpoint of who she was, a very interesting realization occurred to her. In the release, she had a negative epiphany. She exclaimed that her life was a waste. She said, "What a tragedy that I wasted all that time." She spontaneously transferred her "victimization" to a new level. She was angry all over again.

My first response was to continue to follow the energy and unfold the next self-forgiveness, or realization of a false belief. I stopped. My attention was drawn to a "space" on the left side of her head behind her ear. An implant? *Implants* increasingly appear during my sessions with clients. Implants are specialized geometric forms that lock perception into a specific viewpoint. You could say they are thought forms, but they are thought forms placed in the field rather than generated by the person. My awareness of them is subjective; however, acting as if what I perceive is objective works therapeutically.

We can understand implants in the context of Jung's archetypes and the collective unconscious. The difference being that noetic therapy is progressing to a point in which the practitioner can detect subtler levels of the predisposing archetypes. In this case we went from an archetype of (1) *women find their meaning through men and motherhood* to (2) *as a woman my definition is through being a victim*, to (3) *my power is in my self-righteousness and regret about my loss of time when I could have been free* (subtle victim). Rebelling against the archetype is a beginning. However, in the rebelling, one's self-concept continues to be determined by the archetype. Liberation remains elusive.

These "implants" can be cleared by witnessing and consciously naming them to the client, touching them and witnessing, pushing them out by focusing on unconditional love, or dissolving them with a projection of energy, or some combination. However to develop this level of sensitivity and skill, and to follow through in these way, we need a strong ability to *access* higher consciousness.

In this case, I told her to hold that thought, walked over to her and "touched" the implant. The higher spiritual energy of the alignment that I access dissolved it on contact. She took a deep breath and felt a freeing up through her head and chest. Her reality was instantly different. She experienced a sense of freedom and neutrality toward the great "crime against her womanhood." She was no longer perceptually locked into its imprint. Her identification with tragedy instantly became "her watching a movie about tragedy." The implant had locked her perception so that her fulfillment would always be limited by something. "Even if I am free now, I lost those years and can never compensate for them." The implant continued the limiting reality even though she had healed her personal judgments about herself. As long as the implant remained active, there would always be a predisposing force that re-constituted a victim paradigm, insuring the continued formation of victim beliefs. From my perspective, our belief in conflict, or war, is similar.

I grew up with the image that spiritual reality was a divine conflict between good and evil. This was an overlay that was placed onto my experience. The overlay of good and evil shaped the conclusions that I reached about life and meaning. At some point the predisposition began to unravel. The nature of good and evil is illusive and changeable as we change. Our attempt to determine rigid edicts seems to just polarize our reality even more. In our mythology, a war of light and dark began when rebellious angels believed that they were the Source and had no need to rely on anything greater than themselves. By so doing, they lost the awareness that they were larger than their circumstances, even the matrix of their morphogenetic field. It seems to me that this is the same metaphor through which we promote war today. We are not present in our truth, but continue working out a legacy of ancient shadows dancing across the mirror of illusion, acting as if the message is true.

We are always supported in our choice. That is the nature of unconditional love. When we access the field of *living love*, we have the perspective to resolve the duality and use it to manifest and actualize the greater possibilities of self, life and grace. With the *eyes of soul* we can look past the reflective mirror into the field of living love, the formless, the a priori. From that perspective, our adversaries remind us of peace.

There is a law of consequence. The a-priori movement of unconditional love contains a preference for us to return home, to fulfill our nature in love, grace and wholeness. Ah, the treacheries of free will. We forgot our Divine partnership. Our axis of power reversed, and we were no longer anchored in unconditional love and with that reversal, we lost our unlimited access to living energy. The *fall* meant that we must dominate and take energy and resources from others in order to live, predisposing the ultimate rationalization of exploitive business practice and aggressive foreign policy. The commitment to this act decreed that our resources would be limited to that which was already invested in creation. That is, if we persisted.

I concluded then that to engage in conflict, to win by being against, would ultimately create a lose/lose situation. Light battling dark would leave the winner with yet another Source of energy. The shadow of this is that the new Source, no matter how nobly won, would not be renewable. The spoils of conquest, spoil. In a sense, the victor would already be dead.

I am convinced that we are in an *end time* and that we live in a world that is playing out ancient dramas. My client became neutral to the conflict with the removal of an implant (archetype) that she did not create. She may have allowed it or promoted it by falling out of her own grace, but that would have been millennia ago and so entangled with who did what to whom, that we may never find the release by digging for yet one more belief to forgive. Removing her implant changed her relationship to reality such that she was no longer in the "againstness game" of victim/victimizer. Her case is not a standalone example. My conclusion is that "once upon a time" somebody discovered that they could create more resource by placing a program in the genetic morphogenetic field of humanity that limited their perception, and that, by so doing, limited them to the realm of duality by controlling their perception. Once the mind is programmed to perceive life and solutions through the conflict/duality lens, our senses lose the capability of accessing the quantum spheres that hold the true secrets of life. Science then looks into the mirror believing that it is looking into the light. Our highest ethic becomes *justice.* Grace must be "fair." There is nothing wrong with fairness, but when the standard is confined to local evidence, the non-local complement that caused the event remains elusive. Some of us inherit this "gene" more than others. All of us have to break the spell, liberating the paradigm self in service to a yet deeper paradigm that is embedded in our souls, inviting us to be free, impelling us to fulfill our Holiness.

Consider this: As we participate in the drama of this time, we seek grace, enlightenment, going home, spiritual power, and liberation. You name it. This sounds like a good thing. The market place is bustling. Who would consciously choose evil? Who would consciously choose to permanently be a "fallen angel?" By now, we should know that things are often not as they seem. What if, the cause of "light" against "dark," as played out in an adversarial format, is actually a turf war between two different organizations of "dark?" I suggest that there is an *imposter* running through all of this that cajoles the fundamentalist, New Agers, ascensionist and politicos all the same. Each group has its own "buzz" concerning these times.

I have heard that many calamities have been averted that were prophesied because of the great "light work" that we have all done, and continue to do. Makes you feel good. Light work for one group is to conquer the "evil doers." To another group, it is activating your light body and jumping through a star gate. I think that there may be an aspect of truth to all of these. More simple, "light work" is discovering the holy place inside, and using that discovery to transform everything in our growing awareness that is unlike unconditional love. This is what I am calling *access.*

Life is like a movie. When we are caught in the status quo, it is the same as believing we are the movie. From my perspective, more people are choosing out of the practice of defining themselves as being the movie, and aligning with Source as a witnesses to the movie. When we do this we free ourselves from the automatic dictates of the status quo. The drama plays on. *Access* helps us to be aware that we are not the movie.

The deception results in more than our limiting beliefs. The deception goes deeper into the geometry of our consciousness in a way that predisposes us to perceive and choose in terms of duality, separation, and adversity. What causes us to prefer limiting beliefs that act against our Divine Self? To help us understand the dynamic relationship between beliefs and the structural nature of our psyche, we must explore the geometry of consciousness. In ancient terms the study of sacred geometry is similar to our modern view of quantum physics in that they both explain the multidimensional relationship of energy and form.

Beliefs inform the mathematics of the geometry of self. Unity or discord in the structure is a consequence of belief and archetypal forms. The balance in our subtle nature affects our physical health. Through sacred geometry, we can understand the spiritual physics that are the underpinning of Noetic Balancing. As we include the deeper understanding of sacred geometry and spiritual physics in our balancing practice, we enter more directly into the multidimensional aspect of perception and the holographic nature of experience. As we exercise our consciousness in the deeper dimensions of self, we increase our potential for creation based on truth and deception.

As my experience deepens, I look for helpful information in the market place. Briefly, the imposter techniques lock us into the wars of duality at an even deeper level than the implant I discussed earlier. I am not saying that duality is "bad" and wholeness is "good." I am saying that duality embedded in wholeness produces truly healing results. The mission of *Noetic Balancing* is to assist ourselves and others to embrace and resolve duality through living love. This act requires our realism, awareness, commitment, and access to our center and higher consciousness.

Access

Holiness becomes our means of true communication. To accomplish these things, we need *access*, the keys to "heaven." The counterpoint to transforming beliefs occurs through our access to higher consciousness. Through *access* we strengthen our connection to Source, the innate Holiness embedded in our nature, and the cosmic field of the universal noeises.

Our bodies are able to register awareness from all levels of consciousness. We experience this registration as a *felt sense*, *images*, or *holographic awareness*. Once our bodies have an experience of a variance on any dimension, we can then reflect meaningfully on that experience. By variance, I mean the experience of *love, clarity, safety, courage,* etc. By dimension, I mean: *imaginal, emotional, mental, archetypal, soul.* The registered awareness forms a nexus that we then can access spontaneously. Without that nexus, we have great difficulty orienting consciously to the subtleties of our greater consciousness. As long as our conditioning blocks our ability to feel what we are experiencing in our bodies, our sub-conscious, or basic self, does not know how to respond other than telling us that the response we are seeking has no reality for the present scope of our survival. The reason for obscuring individual awareness of the expanded self is to make social control and order easier.

Religious history is based on a tradition of keeping humanity "asleep" to their higher nature in some way. Periodically, someone in that culture, or tribe, has a transcendental experience and articulates his or her higher vision to that group. The vision is either suppressed or embraced. If embraced, over time, the truth of that vision is increasingly replaced by politics, because successive generations cannot maintain the same level of connection. Increasingly, internal access is replaced by external dogma. Eventually, traditions and priesthoods carry too much "baggage" to participate in the reality of enlightenment, even though each person continues to have the capacity to become enlightened.

I have been exploring Noetic Balancing as a therapeutic approach for over forty years. This is not a case of one year of experience repeated forty times. As my connection to *Source* deepens and my grasp of perception pushes into enlightenment, deeper causal levels of why we think like we do become apparent to me. There is something ancient in our genetics and collective unconscious that compels us to re-enforce our perception of duality and to accept conflict as the true and permanent state of our reality.

Beliefs are thought forms that are actual geometric structures that either distort or enhance our balance and the rhythmic exchange between the *source of creation* and our personality. To *access* these beliefs and thought forms, we can open our awareness and directly engage the issues in the unconscious energy field around our bodies. In support of this, *access* anchors transcendent consciousness into our bodies, enabling us to see past our illusions. As we do this, we can "see" into our subconscious and unconscious fields and, by so doing, respond on deeper levels. *Access* itself can resolve karmic forms in our field. It can clear reversals, and it can dissolve static energy.

Freud made us aware that our social and cultural mores caused us to suppress our basic drives. This suppression results in aberrant behaviors toward ourselves and others. Some of these behaviors are collectively condoned and some are not. Jung led us to a deeper view of causality. Great archetypal forces exist in the unconscious that shape the context in which we act and perceive reality. These are the unconscious gods and metaphysical deities of tribal rituals. Lucifer, Satan, and Jehovah are some of the archetypal forces in the

Judeo-Christian tradition. Zeus, Jupiter, and others preside in Greek antiquity. We could go on for pages, listing the equivalent discoveries of people around the globe. In short, Jung grouped all transcendental and extra-terrestrial forces into a band of archetypal forces and beings that have impact on humanity for good or ill. Consider whether the paradigm of right and wrong, good versus evil, them and us, is our certain and continuing reality; or is there an archetype of domination and the law that limits us? One of Jung's most powerful remedies was the integration of opposites, in which we can transcend any duality into a deeper state of individuation. For this reason, I think that wars and conflict are decoys that keep us distracted from discovering the true nature of ourselves and the workings of the universe. There may well be a conflict between "good and evil," but I am not so certain that any useful, or ultimate, answer exists within that paradigm. Having said that, I do consider that the "good/evil" paradigm does raise useful questions.

In the geometric, multi-dimensional space of our body there are key nexus points that readily provide access to psycho-spiritual resources. Whether for personal benefit or for the benefit of others, *access* is essential for our success in using noetic psychology. *Access* aligns us with our innate higher self. The higher self provides the knowing that bridges through eternity and unites us with our multidimensional resources. Because we have loosened the ego identity that we developed through reflections from the mirror of life, we are prepared to explore practices that give us greater spiritual access. By using the following practices, we open and anchor channels of life and energy that are permeated with timeless wisdom. They are the timeless self. As our intimacy with the true self deepens, it dissolves the underlying distortion that creates the pre-disposition for psychological and structural imbalance.

First Access. The first access is through the resolution of limiting beliefs that block and imbalance our energy field, and consciously connecting to the energy movement within our physical body and our personal space. In the body we call this awareness a "felt sense." Around the body, I call it *energy-awareness*, or *spatial seeing*. We "see" as experience.

You begin this access as a journey moving your focus into your loving while moving your awareness into your physical body. Gently reveal to your awareness the tissues, bones, organs and cells of your body. Be aware of your felt-sense while you do this. Take note of the bi-lateral symmetry of your body. See your physical body filled with light as a means of amplifying this process. Remember the principle that life meets you at the level of your understanding and awareness. This is reality. This activity may reveal hidden or sleeping trauma and the associated judgments and beliefs. Forgive yourself for any judgments or limiting beliefs that arise in this process.

Second Access. Now extend your awareness along all surfaces of your skin, and then move your awareness into the space around your body, filling that space to include a sphere, or egg-shape, that extends an arm's length around your body. Identify with this space. It is within this personal space that all psychological dynamics, in the conventional sense, have their location. This is the location of the personal unconscious. The archetypal level is no longer abstract; it is in the space around and in your body. Being present in your space is the second nexus. It is the power of now. Again, forgive yourself for any self judgments or limiting beliefs that you become aware of.

Third Access. We now move to the transcendental access of transpersonal psychology. This is the self that transcends the ego and links with the universe. We find this nexus by directing our perception into a center-line that extends through the geometric center of our spherical space and physical body from the top of our head through our tail bone. Expand this center line to become a tube of light, at least the size of a fisted hand. Now observe your body in your spherical space and the center line column of light as if you were observing the actual geometry. This is perception through imagination. It is using your imagination as a lens. You look through your imagination-eyes at what is present.

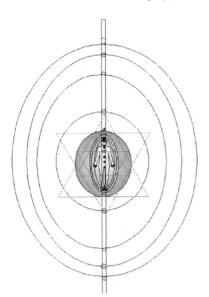

Then, either through your awareness or visualization, place yourself as an image within the central light channel. By so doing, you transport yourself, as consciousness, into this tube as yourself. It is you as your sense of self. With this skill, self is *locatable* to any dimension. You can focus by aligning that sense of identity that is you as an alignment within the tube. You can facilitate this process by seeing an image of a *little you* inside the tube. You are located where you organize your perception to be. This is a locus of intention. This is you as essence using intension as a sense organ. When all else dissolves, your awareness of location is you. When you are aware in a void, you are there. You are not the void. You are your sense of self. Without reassurance of your safety, your ego cannot tolerate the void. If you thought you were the void, you would become afraid of annihilation, because the thought is in the mind, not the void. You can be universally aware of yourself as everything, yet this no-self-self is your awareness of self. As you are one with the void, you will experience peace. This is a key to becoming self as essence.

Now that your sense of self is in the tube, establish this alignment by looking up and down in the tube and see what you see. Sensation is a form of seeing. Since you remain aware in your body and in your space, and, also, in the tube of light, you can say you have bi-located. You are aware in your physical body, your space, and in your center as your sense of self, or soul. In order to consolidate this access, breathe a golden light into the top and bottom of the tube, condensing it in your heart. On the out breath, breathe the light into your body and into your space.

Before we go further, simultaneously hold your attention in your center, your physical body and your space, while relaxing everything. As we add further access, we will also retain awareness of each preceding access. It is like each geometric location is a *locatable* self and is discretely aware and simultaneously aware as a unity.

Fourth Access. Focus in the center of your head. From your vantage point in the center of your head, expand the light in your head into a sphere of light about the size of your head. See yourself walking inside of this ball of light. Move your senses into that image, feeling your buoyancy as you engage this space. As you continue, see yourself walking in nature. Be aware of your feet walking on the earth. Look down at your feet. What are you wearing? Be aware of the sights and sounds: the earth, vegetation, trees, flowers, birds, insects, breeze, etc. What are the sensations and fragrances? Breathe nature through your body.

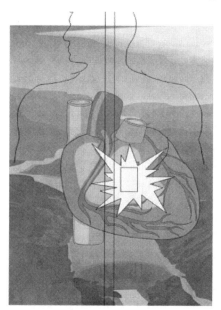

Look up at the sky. Do you see blue sky, clouds, or a night sky filled with stars? Look into the depths of the sky. Breathe in the sky. This journey takes you into your outer heart. Experience the love through Earth and Sky.

Fifth Access. By imagining yourself in nature connected to earth and sky, you cause a change in the field of consciousness that surrounds your body. Through this change in awareness you move your psyche in to a subjective space that I call your *heart space*. In a *quntum* sense, you move your sense of location for your physical body so that it is inside your "heart body."

Now, surrounded by the abundance of your heart-space, look into your physical heart. To make this happen, image that you are seeing as you look. Within the domain of the actual physical heart is a hidden entrance to your sacred heart. Because of trauma and heart-break, we are often cautious of entering our sacred heart. In fact, we may have had so much injury that we have forgotten about the dynamo of loving power within us. It is a Source of love that is beyond duality and, when in force, discontinues adversity. However, we have set the stage and are currently residing in the dynamic geometries of our activated self. Feelings and images may arise of betrayal, disappointment or times when you tried to share your loving and could not. Engage these beliefs and forgive yourself for any self-judgment, limiting beliefs, or beliefs that you are a victim, or are permanently damaged in terms of *matters of the heart*.

See your physical heart, and travel inside. Once inside, ask to be taken into your sacred heart and go with that guidance. You may have a sense of movement, see a small door, or just find yourself there. Once in this space, take in the sights and sounds, becoming oriented to your sacred heart. What do you see, hear, smell? If it is dark you can ask for light, to see, to be shown. This is the space in you that is the "sacred heart of Jesus," or the Sufi "Abode." It is the heart of Hanuman shown in Hinduism. It is here that you meet your inner beloved. Let the atmosphere of this internal place consume you. You are in the expansive realm of your sacred heart. Take your time. When you focus once more into the outer world, you can keep your awareness awake within this space. Be in the world while residing in your *sacred heart* space.

Sixth Access. Now, go to the location in your sacred heart where the golden column of light of your center axis passes through your sacred heart space. When I say go to, this is a true instruction. Your metaphysical location is where your attention is and activates your awareness as genuinely as any physical place. Ask for help if you are having trouble finding it. You cannot make this happen in the willful sense. You can "make" it happen in the *paying attention and relaxing and letting go* sense. You just do it. Your intention will make it so and you will notice more as you practice over time.

While in your sacred heart, stand in the column of light. You may experience it as a vortex of light. This vortex may have a clockwise spin when coming down from above your head, and a counter-clockwise spin when coming from beneath your feet. The orientation of clockwise and counterclockwise is based on you standing on the clock face. Explore whatever experience this nexus presents. Experience the extension of the light through your body, through the geometry of your spherical axis and beyond the space below you. What do you sense or see above you? What do you sense or see below you? Enjoy.

Seventh Access. Travel up the tube, or vortex, out through the top of your physical head. Continue to about a hand's length (six inches) above your head. You will come to a notable space, or place. This is the abode of the high-self. Some people say this is your soul. Certainly, it is a soul-contact. It is a spiritual guide that is a higher aspect of your personality. As you sense this energy, say "show me yourself in a form I can relate to and understand." Say this with intention, love, and anticipation. The form in which it appears may change through continued familiarity and repitition. It will appear as a color, symbol, personification, feeling, or sensation. You might hear a sound or a voice. Engage this energy and establish a dialogue. Dialogue takes many forms, including audible words, images, or a vague sense of some kind of exchange. You begin where you begin. When you activate this nexus, it activates the entire orb around and through your body that is the frequency of the high-self. The high-self will help you practice, so that you can easily repeat this process at each higher level of access. The felt-sense in your body strengthens the high-self connection through the basic-self. As you continue this practice and further exploration, your clarity and center become stronger. By activating the orb of each nexus, the higher energy pushes up through the unconscious, healing and surfacing patterns lodged in the depth of your unconscious.

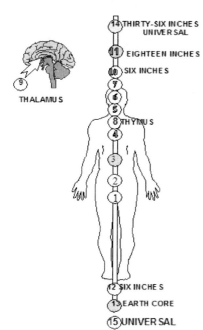

Eighth Access. Continue up the column to at least thirty-six inches. Again, you will sense this location in response to your intention. This is the *Abode* of the Divine Self, or I Am Self. Some people call this your "over soul." It is like an ombudsman in that it knows what to do and where to go for whatever is needed. It is comfortable in your multidimensional self and reality. The protocol is the same. You ask that it appear in a form that you can relate to and understand and go on from there.

This access is on an "as-you-are-ready" basis. As a further empowerment, once you have merged with the divine self, say "Divine Self, activate in every cell, matrix, template, and code of my physical body," and then observe while that process completes itself. Witness, or observation, appears to be necessary in the way perception functions in order for this to work. This access demonstrates that you are truly divine.

Ninth Access. As you continue higher up the light channel, you will encounter another presence. The frequency of your I Am is the entry into the temple of your Master Teacher. In truth it is a higher form of yourself as teacher of your selves. At this level, you encounter yourself beyond time or place. Past and future is a deeper dimension of the present. Follow the previous protocol for engaging and activating the orb associated with this space. This access introduces your senses into an awareness of being cosmic in stature. You are able to access ancient wisdom and cosmic consciousness.

Tenth Access. As you continue up the light channel, you will encounter another presence. This access is the Christ or Christos. It is the template for all that you are and will be. At this level you are encountering an aspect of your nature that is beyond any recent sense of yourself. This is the first taste of fulfilling our Divine destiny in the deepest sense. With this resource you can access the ability and authority to overcome all things. Use the previous protocol to engage, activate and anchor this consciousness. As you observe the action of this access, stay with it for awhile and see where it takes you or what it brings to you.

Eleventh Access. Continue up the vortex, or channel of light, to approximately sixty-seven feet above your head. This is the nexus of the Father/Mother God, the universal one. It is the first contact beyond your personal dimensions, taking you into the universal field of unconditional loving directly, in contrast to filtering it through your own dimensional structure. This is the frequency of your Source as a soul, the primal nature of how you strive to actualize your Holiness through life experience. We have authority on this level to activate and balance our morphogenetic field, sometimes referred to by the ancients as your *crystal body*.

We engage our authority to activate our DNA into its twelve dimensional matrix, resolve past life karma, dissolve limiting core beliefs, and manifest new patterns directly. As we use the protocol to engage and activate this relationship, we are on the true level of our partnership with God. We do all things in partnership. We do our ten per cent and God does its ninety percent. At this level, we have direct access to unconditional love. (See www.thetahealing.com.)

Twelfth Access. Soul Transcendence is the practice of traveling the sound current in your soul body into the a-priori realm, which practically is an unlimited Source of unconditional love. I introduce people to this approach through a simple spiritual exercise composed of chanting and a sound current meditation. This approach has many beneficial spiritual and psychological ramifications.

Chanting is a universal spiritual practice that creates an energy field, or context, and a relationship, based on the intention of the participants. Native American chants and Gregorian chants are examples of our natural understanding that chanting forms a nexus with higher consciousness. In both cases, the focus is devotional, and the rhythms and patterns balance the mind and emotion of the participants and align them with the "Great" or "Holy" Spirit.

We are aware of the effect that music has on our moods. There are spiritual as well as physiological reasons for this. Science and religion have cosmologies that speak of the primordial role of sound in creation. The "big bang" and "in the beginning was the word" imply the seminal role of sound in creation. In the Saurat Shabd Yoga traditions of the mystery teaching, creation unfolds through sound and we return to our spiritual origins through the sound current. We are familiar with inspirational devotional music and its lifting influence. In Shabda Yoga, the adherents chant Sanskrit names of God as a spiritual practice. This practice attunes our constitution to the energy of the sacred sounds, attracts the frequency of the sound current to us, and forms a nexus with it. Specific to this discussion, I use chanting with the group in a particular way.

I like to begin my classes with chanting Ani-Hu. Ani-Hu is a Sanskrit phase meaning "cooperation with God." It promotes the energy of empathy. Sanskrit is an ancient language of archetypal sound. The characters were formed out of what the ancients perceived as the forms made by the sounds. The "names of God," and there are many, attune the practitioner to the transcendental Source of energy represented in the name used. Chanting Ani-Hu is similar to chanting "I love you." Love is the consciousness of Divine cooperation. In this case, it can be our inner child chanting to our higher self, our soul chanting to the All Parent, or the Holiness within us chanting to the Holiness within each of us. In some traditions, Ani-Hu means "I Am." So, the vibration is "I am love," "we are love," or "Love is." Chants such as 'Allah Hoo' (Sufi) resonate to a "God-level," in a similar way to the phrase "hallelujah" (Christian). The spiritual exercise follows a protocol or sequence as follows:

1. As we chant together, we generate a harmonizing, healing and balancing energy that shapes the context we share into a *Holy presence on Holy ground.*
2. As our chanting gains momentum, images and circumstances that are unresolved arise in our individual awareness. Since we are already chanting, we meet the awareness of the unresolved pattern with "cooperation with God" or "I love you." This has a resolving and balancing influence, dissolving miasms and reconstructing limiting beliefs and judgments.
3. As we chant, each person's balance is enhanced and contributes to raising the frequency of the group. In turn, the group, and in-flowing spiritual energy, influence greater healing and balance for individuals in the group.

4. At some point (at least thirty minutes, if it is convenient), we transition from chanting out loud to inner chanting with the *voice* of our mind and heart. With this transition, we focus in, up, and out through the crown chakra. This action promotes a nexus between our Holiness and the sound current, which is an audible life stream of the original Holiness that is the Source of all. In the lineage of "soul-transcendence," we embark on a journey to our spiritual home.
5. We alternately chant and listen, going with the flow of the energy. This flow may draw us upward to higher realms or be in-filling and healing, or both. This pull to higher consciousness is very different from the dissociation of psychological projection; it is the unification of all of the dimensions with Source. This inner practice may require a strong focus of our will into the sound-stream while the business of the mind passes by us, as if we were in a boat on a river of sound watching the mind on the shore. We may at first hear the sound as a silence.
6. Finally, we surrender to the invitation that responds to our chanting, and give ourselves permission to abide with that field of experience, or reality, for awhile. Listen and be heard.
7. After some period of time, we open our eyes and center into our physical bodies. This enfolds heaven and earth together and aligns us from the physical through the soul levels.

This activity creates a unified field: a *sacred ground*, as it applies to our relationship to the earth, and as it applies to the *sacred ground* of the transcendent worlds. The above practice is how I guide the process in my groups. As a personal practice, you may decide to chant out loud for a shorter time, or not at all. You may prefer to move to the inner experience directly. As a personal meditation practice, it is very powerful and may require a time of building the energy for deeper experience. It will have a profound effect on your access.

If you are drawn to this form of meditation, you may want to go beyond this discussion. For years, I have studied with a teacher that offers guidance in this way. It is a deep and ancient teaching of *soul transcendence* and goes far beyond this writing. If you are interested, go to *www.msia.org*. Otherwise, continue practicing the possibilities offered in this writing and go where it leads you. Test everything.

Creating Reality

Now that we have access, an introduction to the geometry of self, awareness of life energy, the nature of perception, phenomenological discovery, and noetic therapy, we are ready for a further step in understanding the dynamic in the *paradigm* self. We are self perpetuating. The good news is that we are eternal. The bad news is that whatever or whomever we have decided that we are, we will perpetuate that self and the environment that supports it.

When we activate our awareness of self in our soul-axis, individuation takes a dramatic turn. Before we became aware of our greater self through access, our transformation was limited to tracking and transforming beliefs as the end-all-and-be-all of the transformational process. Now we are capable of having a personal experience with our higher aspects and with eternity itself. We experience our Holiness in our body through the access of our center.

When we align in, and identify with, the infinite energy of our center, firmly anchored in the earth and Source, a vortex activates that illuminates and draws to it the miasmas of the personal and collective unconscious. By holding our center as a witness and imagining life as the "face of Eternity," drawing *living love* into our space, the miasmas, or forms of distorted creativity, dissolve. There is an old saying that "if you look upon the face of God you will die." As a metaphor, "look upon the face of God, and your false self will die." A new clarity appears in the inner and outer mirror of life. Before, we could see the metaphor of life as it reflected our unconscious back to us through daily living. We lived the paradigm of our tribe or culture. Now, we see a light behind the mirror as if we were meeting our selves coming to us through our life experience, from the horizon of our perception. A light radiates from within that reflects on the mirror and another light that radiates through the mirror from the universal levels of the unconscious. We see this light visually, as sensations, movements, textures, or images, and as sound.

In the following diagram, we can visualize the dynamic action of perception. Perception is a confluence of our personal psychology, genetic makeup, physical constitution, and the metaphysical and spiritual geometries. Through dynamics of perception, we decide the reality that we experience. The double arrows show the projection/reflection of each moment of our breath cycle. Limiting and distorted beliefs pull our awareness away from our center. Our personal psychology exists as if we had no center. Our physical body is the recipient of our self concept. The center exists, but for all practical purposes, it exists abstractly. The reinforcement cycle of perception bases reality on our physical body. Consequently, we perceive our body and our space as our total reality.

Continuing with our exploration of the unconscious mind, as the space in which our physical body is nested, we can form a picture of how levels of personal, cultural, and natural history form levels of perception that limit and distort our experience. Common sense tells us there is a deeper implicate order from which an undistorted template of self once emerged. This template is the Source of our motivation to fulfill our true nature through the challenges of our lives.

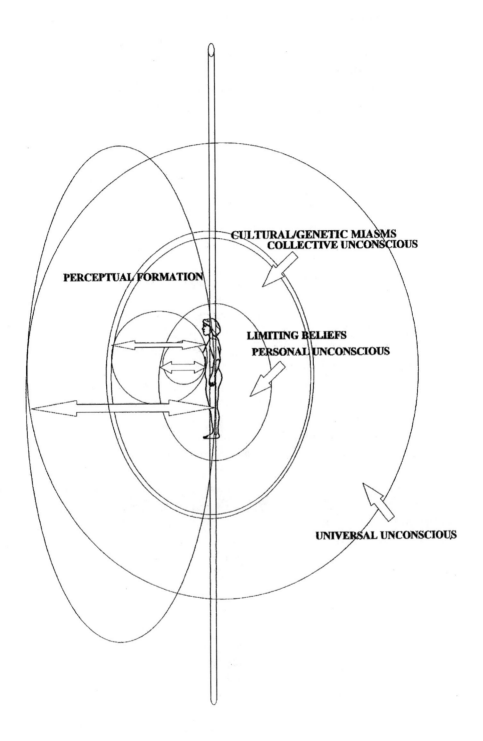

Close at hand are the personal beliefs that we formed from our responses to the situations and circumstances of our lives. Of concern are the beliefs that limit and distort the picture of our self from the truth or essence of who we are. From a Buddhist sense, this self is a no-self, and that is compatible with this discussion, because the ego, based on duality, dissolves into a non-dual experience, which we experience as everything and self.

The coding for truth or essence can be accessed through our center or soul axis. When we wake-up in the center, we can access the flow of energy that carries these codes. We become able to inform our selves inwardly of our true nature. This occurs beyond "our truth" as truth itself. The central flow of energy also enables us to resolve distortions by bringing the higher information, as energy, into the lower.

Beneath the frequency of our own created beliefs is the underlying influence of the collective unconscious. Each of the fields encompasses and interpenetrates the field below it. In like manner, our perception is sustained through the projection/reflection cycle. The thought forms of the collective cause a predisposition to think, choose and act in certain ways. Classic limiting phrases from the collective are:

> You know your worth through comparison to others.
> You are innately bad or unworthy.
> When you do good you are good.
> When you do bad you are bad.
> Women find their value through men.
> To be safe we have to control resources and dominate others.
> Redemption is external.
> Men find their value through rescuing women.
> Consciousness emerges from physical evolution.
> Etcetera.

A list like this can go on and on. As individuals, we can list the phrases that underlie and are foundational to our approach to life. These patterns are ancient and permeate our human existence whether we participated in their creation or not. These beliefs often dissolve when we are actively centered and bring them into our awareness. In order to dissolve personal beliefs, we must incorporate some form of self-forgiveness or experience an epiphany that reveals our divine self in relationship to the thought forms created by the limiting beliefs.

As we resolve the miasmas of the personal and collective unconscious, our conscious self expands beyond the duality of these levels. As the experience of a non-dual unity of these various forces of life emerges, the barrier between the distortions of the collective and personal levels dissolves and the original pattern of human health merges within all of our levels and expressions and we spontaneously and progressively correct ourselves.

Rudolf Steiner observed that our soul approaches from the horizon. When our perception is limited to the personal and collective unconscious, reality reinforces our beliefs as true. Life appears to us as a "small" physical world oriented to our body. As we expand beyond this limitation in our noetic field, our reality field dissolves the patterns and codes that produce distortion and limitation. We see truth directly. As Paul said: "I look through a glass darkly, yet face to face."

Conventional psychology effectively explores our issues and needs through finding and correcting beliefs and trauma produced developmentally along our time line. This is an effective therapeutic approach. It becomes more effective as we experientially identify with our center and expand that light to encompass our body, mind and emotions. As we increasingly identify with center and reach up and affiliate our sense of self with higher archetypal and spiritual levels of self, we reverse the trends of our negative, reversed creations. By that, I mean that as we stand in the presence of our truth and light, and identify with it, our shadow is pulled into the light. Searching the dark corners of our developmental traumas becomes much easier when the traumas and their constellated beliefs are pulled into the light.

The force propelling this process is our core impetus to actualize. All of our creations and adopted creations seek actualization. Because of that, we fulfill them by either completing the consequence of that choice or pulling our essence out of the distortion, thereby restoring our self to our self. This is the "It of Itself." When we find ourselves in the non-dual experience of universal love, we declare in that moment: "This I am." Individuation is complete, and the boundary of our separated self dissolves.

The practice of spiritual psychology, whether on our own behalf or on behalf of others, requires us to move to a heightened state. Preparation is continual. As healers, we are evolving a self based on a center of universal intelligence, contained in the encompassing field of universal love. To do this, we reach into our center and out to the universal field. As we do this, an inductive response occurs in our selves, or others with whom we are working, that stirs a remembrance of essence. In this way all therapeutic forms are enhanced by our perceptual state. The shadow is called forward into the light.

Living Love

Everything is conscious. That is why we say *living love*. We can generate love, because we are love; however, love generates because love of itself knows how. We generate love through our relationship with love. When we subject love to conditions, we are reversing love to something less, something contained or stored within us that can no longer replenish itself. Love is the law of attraction. When it is primal love, the creation is attracted to itself. When it is conditional, we are attracted through the karmic law of love. Like attracts like. We get what we love. If we love conditionally, we get conditional love.

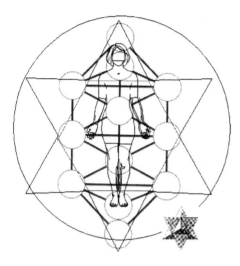

This discussion has a twofold purpose. *One* is to reconcile our nature through conversion. By this I mean that our life blood is *living love*. When we center, we activate a circulatory system that appears as a *body of light*. The ancients called this the merkaba. It can be as simple as that. The manifestation of *living love* purifies and activates health in all of our systems. *Two* is that, as we reflect on the geometry of self, we awaken deep structures that promote health, that are health.

Light Body

When we chant the ancient Sanskrit ANI-HU with an intention to move our awareness into Source, empowered by unconditional love, we also purify the morphogenetic field. The ancients understood that a matrix in each dimension of the morphogenetic field encodes the information from which form manifest. They call this matrix the Kathara. The Light Body is the circulatory system of the Kathara, translating energy and information from the morphogenetic field into the physical body. This is the linkage between our spiritual nature and our DNA. The light body is also called the Merkaba.

This is a very simplistic view of our entire cosmology; however, it is the pattern, and the other dimensions harmonically respond in kind as we awaken to ourselves in this way. The light body structure functions as a star tetrahedron which consists of two interwoven, counter rotating tetrahedrons. As seen, the light body is symbolized by a six pointed star. This symbol appears universally in many wisdom teachings around the planet. These counter rotating electromagnetic spirals form as a natural consequence of the merging multidimensional spirals. All forms are created through sets of merkaba spirals.

Merkaba spirals draw energy and consciousness from the dimensional unified fields, through the central axis from Source, into the morphogenetic field (form holding blue print), feeding a continual supply of energetic substance into the blue print from which particles build up to create manifestation of that blue print into matter. Merkaba spirals bring into being. This action is aligned through the central flow channel to the Christos, soul axis.

Merkaba fields are the energy engines and consciousness carriers by which life force and Consciousness are circulated between the internal Kathara Grid (morphogenetic field) template and the ionic particles as they pass into and out of external expression. These are the spheres of influence for each light/sound dimensional level. These spheres correspond to the levels of consciousness.

Fantasy

With each breath, we compute our existence. In a multidimensional instant our form, the universe we are in, and the gestalt of our beliefs coalesce into the holographic perception that makes our reality in this moment what it is. We have been doing this our entire life. When we change a belief, our reality changes. When we change a core belief, our reality changes a lot. The value of Noetic Balancing is that people can transform more rapidly.

Early in our lives, we formulate a perspective of ourselves that mediates who we are and who we are living with. This often requires us to design our ego, our self concept, with components that are based on those around us in our families, our communities and nations. This is good because in helps us live, survive, and even thrive. However, the selves based on such information can create fantasy realities. Our basic selves pick up the pattern of this information and project a transcendental sphere that replicates the information as if it is true. We pray to deities that only have an existence in the fantasy heaven of our group consciousness. We make up a story about our lives and live it as if it is true. Perhaps any life story has the quality of fantasy.

During a balancing, the fabric of these fantasy realities is systematically undone. When the distinction between the real and the fantasy is evident, we become aware of the frequency in the noetic field. This in itself is often enough to dissolve the fantasy field. One of the ways I have experienced this energy is as a feeling of "Novocain." I make an association to the numbing sensation of the dentist chair. So, we each develop a sense or sensitivity to the frequency of fantasy fields. When we sense this, we bring it to awareness and usually that provides the opportunity for the light to disperse this field.

These fields compete with the higher alignment of the noetic field. The imaginal, emotional and mental fields can participate in the fantasy alignment and to some extent activate the flow of energy through the Light Body on those levels, but the morphogenetic field becomes infiltrated with false information and this can shift our sense of reality so that the false seems real and the unhealthy is believed healthy. In this way, our life field becomes reversed, and we adapt. The morphogenetic field of the fantasy will substitute for the formative information of our blue print. We could say that the fantasy influence compromises the Kathara matrix. Because of the substitution of fantasy thought, our experience of higher consciousness will be false and limited. We will lose awareness to the genuine experience of higher states of consciousness.

Sometimes these fields are held in place by implanted thought forms that operate out of a transcendental host that the individual has had associations with in the past. In those cases there is an oath, pledge, initiation, contract or agreement that was made in exchange for some hoped-for gain. Often these patterns appear in the present as conditional love, which is love based on fear. We have to behave or believe in a certain way to get the love we need from someone else.

When we expand out into the subtle worlds, we encounter a field of dreams. Perhaps some of these dreams were meant for manifestation and grounding into physical reality, often enough, they are collective formations that may have once given us a sense of reality but are incompatible with the present, so we live in the past. Other dreams are more tragic because these fantasies are meant to escape into a never-never land. The more sinister dreams manifest into an imposter reality, whether on this plan or another. Then there are the ones that delude our aspirations for higher consciousness. In these fantasies, we dream up a spiritual reality, and then "discover" within it an imitation, or imposter, enlightenment or devotion. We enshroud ourselves in an imitational righteousness.

Most fantasies dissolve when made clear in the light of a strong spiritual witness, like when friends who love us call us on the ways we fool and delude ourselves. However, when our friends collude, our fantasies become consensus and may take a catastrophic disappointment to resolve. The greatest remedy for these imitations of life is *living love*. When we align with the manifestation of *living love*, the false fields convert to the soul standards and the fantasy manifestation dissolves or depolarizes with truth.

Chapter Four

ESSENTIAL UNDERSTANDING

The reality of self as a conscious energy field is essential to the understanding and the effective application of Noetic Balancing and how it fits into the range of cosmologies from which we guide the various ways we serve ourselves and others to develop healthy realities. This energy, though nonphysical, has a form of substance particular to the realm one is accessing. Equally helpful is our capacity to metaphorically extrapolate the models of physics. Though it is clear that the energy of physics is different from that of metaphysics, there is value in the symbolic connection of the two. However, from the perspective of quantum physics, the difference in the two energies is less clear. Whatever the case, the concept of "energy" helps us articulate the noetic experiences. Just as the atom is theoretically inferred based on its effects, we can infer the soul based on its mental, emotional, and physical effects. Though our technology has not yet given us vision into the atom, with spiritual sight, we can see into the world of the soul. Through *eyes made of soul*, we can look into the universe of the atom and know where to direct our technology and how to interpret the information we gather. As we unlock our soul vision, we find that we are also able to sense and interpret changes in this energy field through the interface of the dense and subtle forms of our nervous system and to perceive nonphysical realms. I suspect that at some point, we will discover that the energy of physics and metaphysics is the same.

NOETIC FIELD MODEL

All noetic protocols begin with a prayer (silent or spoken) and an alignment with higher consciousness. As an enhanced form of rapport, the client enters the noetic field with the practitioner. This constitutes a shift into an altered state of consciousness that enhances the client's ability to access appropriate information, clarity, and forgiveness. The client may not be aware of this shift, so the practitioner must be adept at holding a witness, alignment, and focus. As the noetic field becomes more energized, the interface and the nexus points expand to include all senses, one or more inner senses, and Higher Sense Perception (HSP). In some ways, our entire consciousness and somatic sensitivity become avenues of perception.

Nexus Points

There are many nexus points. We will explore two in this discussion. One is the nexus to the noetic field. The other is within the therapeutic relationship. The nexus point that connects to higher consciousness is in the top of the head, while the nexus that engages the energy field of the client is in the forehead and often tracks with the physical vision and HSP. The forehead nexus is *attention,* and the top of the head nexus is *intention.* You maintain a simultaneous attentiveness with these nexus points while interacting with the therapeutic process as it presents itself. When using the forehead point in this way, be careful not to project into the field of the client. That action will tend to enmesh you in the client's energy, making it harder to maintain clear alignment and may confuse your energy and cause "compassion fatigue," or promote "counter-transference." If your projection is overwhelming to the client or simply gives a sense of invasion, she or he will be protective and want to move away from you.

The development of the nexus points is important to your ability to use this therapy effectively. If this is an unfamiliar or uncomfortable viewpoint, you need not assume your nexus points are not active, or that you lack aptitude or skill. A variety of religious, spiritual, counseling, and ethical practices promote the development of these points. Developing the observer, unconditional positive regard, rapport, intuition, phenomenological reduction, and transforming one's countertransference all support the development of these centers. Years of impeccable experience based on spiritual values will enhance your development. Noetic Balancing calls for the initiation of conscious, concerted attention to awakening, aligning, and centering in your soul-space; practicing Noetic Balancing protocols; and doing regular spiritual practices.

Dynamics

The following diagram charts the noetic relationship between the client and therapist. It can also be taken as a diagram of the relationship between any two people interested in assisting each other to transform a problematical situation or limiting belief. This is a dynamic relationship that brackets all, including the client and therapist.

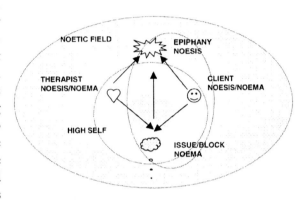

As a helping person, your witness and alignment is essential, because you must also deconstruct your own process, including all beliefs and constructs concerning what you know or who you are and what you are doing, while at the same time remaining engaged with higher consciousness and the client.

While the client deconstructs the sedimented belief (block/noema), you deconstruct any countertransference (noema) including your equivalent of the client's issue. The epiphany occurs when the client accesses the noetic field through the focus of the client's issue (block). The practitioner's alignment and impeccability enhance the transformative experience.

The noetic field is accessed by the relationship of the practitioner, client, and higher consciousness. The noetic field is the basis for the learning and the therapeutic experience. The field is initiated by the connection of your focus, and increases in subtlety and power as the therapeutic process proceeds. Once the access to the noetic field is experientially created between you and the client, a realization emerges that the noetic field already existed as an infinite resource. Since this is an experiential discovery, you may have to accept the assertion that it works on faith. It will work, and, at some point, the experiential validation will emerge.

Enfolding and Unfolding Holiness

Our place, and the space it circumscribes, is our *sphere of influence*. We enfold time, as we live it, into an implicate order of our place. The past is an implicate dimension of the present. In the geometrical context of self awareness as place, we are implicated in a greater presence of a transpersonal self, a soul-self. Our soul implicates and transcends our time bound self as spatial context. This is the essence of transformation.

Through the vehicle of self, we can unfold specific implicate realms within. We can all enfold our awareness into these inner dimensions. Self as nexus is our gateway to our inner worlds. We begin to develop these aspects of self while exploring the inner dimensions of self, as holy space, as inner teacher. In our wholeness, our footprints appear in all times and places at once.

HIGHER SENSE PERCEPTION

Higher Sense Perception (HSP) presents a gentle view of the expanded scope of your ability to see, feel, hear, speak, and touch. The media presents us with a wide range of views as to what HSP might be. From documentaries to the "X-Files" to *Escape to Witch Mountain*, our imagination is enticed or repulsed. HSP might be all these things. Regardless of what it is, you must begin where you are. You are a doorway to deepen and expand your awareness. Fundamentalist viewpoints call HSP "the devil," and then accommodate spiritual information by saying "God told me," or "God wants me to _____." Perhaps the "devil" is in the politics. Having said that, always test the experience and information that you get through HSP and God. Some agendas may not be for the highest good even though they look like God. Any unresolved agenda that you may have, to compensate for inadequacies or use your service to manipulate others, can make you receptive to the imposters of higher consciousness that seem like the true God, angels and guides, but, like you, have a hidden agenda.

Many actually see the energy of the aura. What they see varies, but all the accounts include the description of colors and forms surrounding the body. The colors range from muddy and dull to bright and clear. The forms range from grotesque and degenerate to lofty and divine. There are many carefully written books that describe and explain the appearance of the aura and how it looks when it is in balance or out of balance. These references discuss at length the thought forms and psychological patterns that can exist in the aura.

I prefer to begin with touch, perception, and inner awareness. In my experience, approaching it in this way is easier, more familiar, and connects more readily to our already developed use of the five senses. I also use a pendulum as a reflective and focusing instrument. I also insist on the concurrent or prerequisite development and strengthening of one's character and spiritual center.

The phenomenon of noetic balancing is enticing. My concern is that as you learn and explore this wonderful technique, it must remain an extension of your Holiness and not become a force that shapes or inhibits your sense of self. In learning Noetic Field Balancing, as in all things, your first priority must be to shape yourself from your divine nature and through your relationship with God.

Touch

Touch is very familiar. We feel temperature, pressure, and textures and receive and convey warmth. We have the "reach-out-and-touch-someone" people and we have the "don't-touch-me people." Touch fills our vocabulary with a wisdom that tells us that we already participate with life through HSP. We "touch the sky" or we are "touched by beauty"; a story or a demonstration of compassion or courage is "touching." Our sense of touch includes our body, imagination, emotions, mind, and spirit. Energy awareness provides acuity to our touch. Energy is touch and is the media that makes all the expressions of touch possible.

Hands are a primary instrument of touch and transmission of energy. Hands are so highly developed that if they were the only instrument we had to do balancing, it would be enough. With our hands we can find the blocks, hold a focus and conduct energy.

Awareness is selective. We have been trained all our lives to be selective in the sensations we allow ourselves to be aware of. This skill gives us clarity and delineation in our lives. It makes life manageable and facilitates our communication with family and community. Now we need to use that selectivity in conjunction with sensing the variations of energy in the field. Your physical hand, etheric hand, and nervous system join as you pay attention to the energy near the palms of your hands. Remember, pay attention and relax.

First Skill. The first skill of touching is, when you slowly pass your hand through another person's field, to register variations in the energy fields, such as heat, density, or texture. On the physical level, it feels course, granny, warm, cold, sticky, or thick. On the emotional level, you might feel sadness, joy, loneliness, love, jealousy, or kindness. On the mental level, you have viewpoints and attitudes. Couple mental touching with inner seeing. Allow yourself to see images, impressions, or stories in your mind while perceiving into the client's consciousness through touch. Archetypal touching is much like mental touching only much more vast and expansive. Archetypes carry destiny. Usually, if we feel the archetypal level, it is already in a process of changing. Generally, you will not need information to balance that energy.

Second Skill. The second skill of touching, then, is to select the level of energy we want to touch. This is done by intention and bracketing your focus. *Bracketing* is the practice of excluding everything from your field of awareness other than the focus of you interest. When you focus selectively on the emotional aura, that is what you will detect. A change in focus changes the frequency to the level of information you want. Again, by changing your focus to the physical aura, that is what you will detect.

Third Skill. The third skill occurs as a second level of awareness that rides in across the first and provides information in the form of images, inner knowing, or seeing.

Perception

Perception is a psychological, physical, and spiritual process. Respect your perception and never take it for granted. It is like an organ that develops with experience. Learn to see and interpret the world around you; then, the world within you; and then, differentiate between the two. Perception is selective, which is its greatest strength and its greatest weakness.

Rudolf Steiner spoke of developing the mind as a sense organ of perception. What is it like to see with the mind in contrast to limiting the mind to only thinking? We want to know the purpose of the phenomenon. When we know its purpose, we can facilitate its wholeness. Everything moves toward fulfilling its nature. Every action initiated seeks completion. When we look in this way at something, it will reveal itself to us. It will tell us the truth. When we look with an agenda, we cannot see the truth. We see the agenda and call it the truth. Perception is a complex relationship that produces the holographic sense of reality in which we function at any given place or time.

Inner Awareness

Inner awareness begins with your first sense that you are a reality that is distinct from your surroundings. It is complete when you have the awareness that you are one with everything. Engage with your touch and surrender to your inner awareness. Inner awareness includes all psychological, psychic, and spiritual levels. As a practitioner, your goal is to develop your soul-space such that it mediates your inner awareness.

In your soul-space, the only agenda resides in the unconditional, universal love that you experience as a divine presence. This presence is an energy that is life, knowing, and intelligence. It is the noetic field. Action and understanding the action are not separate. Through inner awareness, you can simultaneously learn and do. This is desirable because of the variety of human nature and expression. Each awareness is an individualized experience of the universal. It is the separating belief that must be balanced.

Practice of Observing

When you hear the word *observing*, do you first think only visual? From the perspective of soul seeing and noetics, *seeing* is also hearing, sensing, apprehending, and knowing. As a practice of *Student's Mind*, we can open the observing faculty through the practice of listening.

The context for witness is generally set in place through seeing as an outward observation while simultaneously looking inwardly through our center light column, and anchoring into the light form in the center of the earth and up into the highest heaven. When we complement this with listening, a resource begins to link us into the sound current.

We look outward and listen while we talk and the client talks. We look inward and listen. This occurs through a geometric focusing into center. This action opens our perception. All of us may not at first be clairvoyant. When we practice listening, a sphere of seeing activates in our presence, in our space, in our noegenesis. It is somewhat vague or dim at first, and then with use it grows brighter. This is akin to the statement of Paul in the Bible: "I see through a glass darkly, then face to face." We experience a global phenomenon in which we see images and pictures. This is an altered state in which we see through experiencing the reality of perception.

Further activation occurs by extending our hearing into our seeing. For example, you see a waterfall as a silent image, at first. As you watch, you hear or imagine the sound of a waterfall. This activates the sound dimension. When that occurs, you can hear, also. You have a nexus into the sound current. For another example, imagine a flock of geese flying overhead. Hear the geese. Hear the wind passing through their wings. Soon you are traveling with them. You feel the group support of the air lifting your body. Your soul eyes open.

PENDULUM

In my experience, many people, including people who use them, take a superstitious approach to the pendulum. The pendulum is not magical. It is neither good nor evil. It is a neutral instrument that responds to subtle physical movement, intention, and thought. The pendulum also appears to respond to psychic and spiritual movement. It is not always clear, however, whether it is responding directly to these subtle energies or whether the physical body is registering these subtle energies amplifying them through the mechanical nature of the pendulum. The issue is not whether or not energy moves the pendulum. You develop the skill and understanding of the pendulum so that you can effectively help the client. Depending on the consciousness and skill of the practitioner, the pendulum is an excellent instrument when used in the appropriate context for the appropriate needs.

As used in Noetic Balancing, The pendulum focuses and objectifies subtle energy. It is a conduit for energy and can reflect information. Discipline and impeccability are the keys to its usefulness. In a manner of speaking, your potential to use the pendulum therapeutically is like your ability to speak. When your potential to speak is overlaid by and given language, you are able to communicate. In other words, the pendulum provides a focus, a nexus. By holding your attention on the pendulum, a locality opens, providing a gate through which the unfolding and enfolding of the implicate and explicate orders are enhanced. This facilitates the reordering of the blocking or unbalancing structure.

The action of the pendulum is very sensitive to your focus, thought, and imagination. You can visualize the pendulum spinning clockwise, and it will do so. There is no dogma or set way the pendulum spins that always means the same thing. Use it to explore the patterns of energy, and use those observations descriptively, not interpretatively. When doing Noetic Balancing, you are not visualizing or telling it how to spin.

When I teach the use of the pendulum, we establish a convention, a neutral pattern that governs the basic pattern of its movement. We can then observe the pendulum and know what is going on. Keep it simple. Movement means something is there to balance. For example, Clockwise rotation means balancing is occurring. Stillness means the balancing is finished. The convention is to give the basic self a reference which allows spirit to unfold and assist for the highest good. The basic self needs the ritual. Spirit needs the connection. Counter clockwise in this convention occurs less often, and indicates that energy is drawing out. When the pendulum is above the head on a central axis or below the feet, a counter clockwise spin may indicate directional energy flow. Once you establish the convention, you intention selects the convention, but does not direct the spin.

The implicit controversy that goes with the pendulum is helpful, because it reminds us to be vigilant and always test our perception. The slightest pull toward power moves our intellect away from discerning love. The slightest fear makes our loving kindness toxic. Established as a convention, the oscillation reflects enfolding and unfolding holomovement between the implicate and explicate order. This description may be taking liberty with Bohm's quantum model. However, there is a kinship. Noetic field theory and quantum theory unfold from the same implicate reality. The block itself is an unfolded localization phenomenon of a distorted field. The pendulum assisted focus, facilitates a loosening of the beliefs that are sedimenting the distortion.

Other models of energy may produce different results. Our own perceptions shape the given reality, and shape the reflective event. For example, when earth magnetism is the focus the pendulum may respond differently than when the dimensional interaction between form and essence is the focus. Rotation may have a different impact than when the convention reflects a quantum perspective. In a quantum model matter is contained in a multidimensional implicate order. The polarization of localized distinctions is not the focus. The focus is on the relationship of the localized distinction and the shared implicate reality. Said another way, the distinction is between the soul's intention and the created belief. Balancing is approached from the soul. If one is approaching the block from the perspective of the Earth, the pendulum may rotate in terms of the earth reference. For example, it may rotate counter-clockwise in one convention and clockwise in another.

From the perspective of distinctions, the rotation may need to be exact because of how the impact on the integrity of the energy field is understood. From the explicate, magnetic viewpoint, a counter-clockwise rotation for balancing and closing the aura may be essential because the earth is negative in relationship to spirit, rather than earth being explicate to spirit.

This is all very interesting. It is the *stuff* of investigation and developing understanding. These considerations will last for years. In the meantime, a practical approach is needed. I suggest to my students that they use the convention that I call the *standard procedure*, as a guide to the basic self and connection for spirit, and then continue to develop their skill of intuitive responsiveness and reflective checking. I discussed this topic in an earlier chapter.

Another dimension of this discussion asks: does the rotation cause the balancing activity or does the focus of intention loosen the structure so that the enfolding/unfolding dynamic is enabled? In the first case, the pendulum is an instrument of causation. In the second case, the pendulum is an instrument of focus that reflects the implication and explication. The intention I teach is to *connect*, and *serve*. It is not an intention to balance, per se.

I also caution you to be careful when practicing with the pendulum. Depending on your attitude, your focus with the pendulum can randomly open the energy field and centers, and even transmit agendas. One function of the aura is to protect the psychological and physical bodies from the thoughts and projections of others. Always take care to close any aspect of the aura that you have opened.

Like any good accounting system, I also teach a way of checking information by using the pendulum as a dowsing tool. For example, when you see something inwardly, you may get a psychic impression, or sense something. Check this information by holding the pendulum in one hand and suspending it over the index knuckle of the other hand. The knuckle hand is held as a loosely closed fist with the knuckle pointing up. The interpretive convention is that clockwise means "yes" and counter clockwise means "no." Proceed by asking a yes or no question. When the two answers are the same, the information is more reliable. When they are different, the information is suspect. The best method, of course, is to check the information with the client. If it resonates with them, it has validity. In any case, our motive is to draw out the truth from our clients and avoid overlaying our external interpretation onto them, no matter how inspired.

Also, I find it helpful to periodically step back from the client and realign myself and establish my center. I disconnect momentarily and focus my awareness in my soul-space. Through my soul-space, I focus on my alignment with the Holy Spirit and pray for a clearing of any way or any level of interference that may be impinging or competing with the therapeutic process. For these purposes, it is not important whether the interference originates within ourselves or externally; the results are the same. When I sense the clearing and alignment has occurred, I silently re-engage the client and continue.

SELF FORGIVENESS

There are three fundamental levels to Noetic Balancing: *physical*, *emotional*, and *mental-spiritual*. When we engage the mental-spiritual level with the pendulum, we engage the client verbally as a means of drawing out, clarifying, and facilitating balance. Each block, at some level, carries a damaging belief about one's self. We formulate these beliefs in response to situations and circumstances in our lives. Self-forgiveness is a trigger to release self-judgment, which ultimately includes any judgment.

Semantics are a key ingredient in the client's ability to disclose and forgive. We often have to discover the phrases and concepts of self-judgment and self-forgiveness that are indigenous to the client.

Phineus Parkhurst Quimby

Phineus Parkhust Quimby practiced in the mid and late 19th century. The concept of self-forgiveness used in the context of this book came from Quimby's approach, which gained its most powerful expression with patients who didn't respond to the allopathic medicine practiced at that time. His approach to healing was based on the interaction of three dynamic forces contained within the client and two elements provided by the practitioner. The forces within the client: inner Christ, belief, and self-forgiveness. The elements within the practitioner: witness and channel. The interaction of these forces and elements created the context through which the universal spirit or power provided by God could accomplish the work.

Inner Christ. The inner Christ is a health-giving spiritual form. Though Quimby originally derived this term from the Christianity of his day, his experience as a healer caused him to expand his understanding to incorporate a more universal meaning. As a universal form within humanity, the Christ came to mean the individual extension of a universal form of divine energy. It is also archetypal, as it translates its presence into our individual and collective expression. This energy field motivates us to seek its actualization. It is the encompassing authority in our personality and the driving motivation of our daily acts. The Christ is also the formless energy that generates and provides the boundless inspiration and vitalizing power channeled by the archetype. For Quimby, the Christ came to mean the pattern of our destiny and the force of energy that empowers and sustains our fulfillment as a living experience.

Belief. To Quimby, belief can be an obstacle to the healing flow of the Christ energy. Beliefs form the foundation of health by enhancing or blocking our natural propensity to heal. Beliefs that exclude the inner Christ cause dis-ease (disturbing our ease). Essentially, any belief that forms the basis of a judgment against self as good and divine is false and makes one receptive to illness.

Self-Forgiveness. Self-forgiveness is essential for healing. Since God does not violate itself and gives humanity freedom of choice, God does not force us to have health if we choose otherwise. We are, however, responsible for the consequences of our actions as choices. It is not so much that we make the illness or make ourselves sick; it is more that we limit our capacity to heal or receive healing. We reap what we sow. In the context of Quimby's teaching, self-forgiveness allows the healing power to flow through us and transform dis-ease.

When Quimby explained the nature of dis-ease and reviewed the imbalancing and blocking beliefs held by his patients, his purpose was to make them receptive to healing through forgiving themselves for the beliefs and judgments that were created through their own volition. As his patients accepted that truth was a Source of consciousness beyond their belief—not belief itself—and that dis-ease developed from an error in thinking, they enabled their own transformation. Self-forgiveness instructs the *basic self* to change, and invites the *high self* to promote change. This is important because in regard to our formed beliefs, spirit is unconditional love and will not violate the choice of another Divine being.

Witness and Channel. When Quimby held witness, he became a conduit or channel for divine energy or a presence that collapsed the programming. As witness, he beheld and affirmed the Christ within them. This act facilitated the awareness within his clients of the truth of their inner power. Quimby, in his silent alignment, enhanced the healing energy. This was possible because his patients were willing to give up their judgments against themselves and accept the health-giving presence of the inner Christ. He was also present as the Christ within himself.

Energy Blocks

Blocks in a client's field are created in response to:

- trauma;
- thwarted attempts to share loving, enthusiasm, or joy;
- thwarted attempts to be nurtured or cared for;
- the status quo of the respective culture;
- the human condition;
- authoritarian patterns in the collective;
- genetic and family heritage;
- drug use;
- environmental imbalance;
- pledges, agreements, initiations, oaths and curses.

It is in our nature to seek new experience and then transform that experience into understanding, strength, and awareness. Blocks are a natural increment of human destiny. Blocks are created as an adaptive response to challenging, frightening or painful encounters.

We block ourselves through attaching ourselves to substances and beliefs that are an antithesis to our essence. We judge ourselves in terms of intuited spiritual truths, the imprint of our destiny, and developed or acquired standards. At times, our choices, lifestyle, or circumstances severely deplete our life force. If that is the case, the life force (chi, prana) must be increased sufficiently for us to respond to the energies of the imagination, emotion, mind, unconscious, soul, and spirit. Awareness balances omissions, and forgiveness balances commissions.

Application

In self-forgiveness, look for and find the moment that clients chose against themselves during the experience of trauma. As they connect with the traumatic moment and forgive themselves, they are changing the beliefs and self-definitions they formed at that time. Their rationalization of the event is transformed.

Because of our sophistication and cultural diversity, you must have a deep understanding of the subtle nuances of judgment and forgiveness. Clients' instinct to protect will most likely respond adversarially when a strongly held belief, such as their self-concept, is challenged. This is natural. A sophisticated mind will debate subtlety to avoid simply engaging the hurt and forgiving the damaging aftermath. The psychological damage is our own doing. What to do with the perpetrator is another issue entirely and best comes after we have healed ourselves. Resistance in the client often reflects that we have not resolved the same issue.

Whatever the culture, we can develop shame, blame, and guilt from acts that go against cultural norms or violate taboos. Even accepted values may promote a distortion about human goodness or inherent unworthiness. Because we are human, we are inherently pushed toward goodness and wholeness. When we fail our standards, we must find a reason. Sometimes that alleged reason is that we are a bad person. Whether we use "I forgive myself for . . ." or not, we still need to transform the act against self. You must pursue the nature of judgment and forgiveness relative to the person.

In most cases, to transform the block, the individual needs to hear his or her own spoken words say, "I forgive myself." This is not to say self-judgment cannot be conceptualized many ways or that self-forgiveness cannot be said or done in many ways. It can. Explore the best way to proceed. Just as we can be too dogmatic about the literal practice of self-forgiveness, we can also become too dogmatic against it. Dogma of any kind moves into polarization. In this sense, dogma is an act against one's own Holiness. Self-forgiveness dissolves the separation, and dogma gives way to the whole spirit.

When you search for an effective dialogue for self-forgiveness, listening is a key. Listening reveals subtle nuances in the sound of the voice that reflect judgment regardless of culture. Also, there are universal judgments that stem from our common human encounter with life. Most cultures have a form of dominating others, a less-than/more-than mechanism. Both of these positions separate ego from self or self-concept from one's Holiness. The more shame-based the culture, the harder it may be for a person to accept their own authority to exercise self-forgiveness. Beliefs and feelings that we are too unworthy to forgive ourselves will stop us. Cynicism closes the heart to the mind; consequently we lose the information stream of love. With our affair with what-ifs and yes-buts, we diffuse the ability of our minds to respond.

The guideline is to look for how that person in that culture diminishes the Holiness of self or separates from the inherent goodness of self that forms the belief or judgment dimension of forgiveness. Self-forgiveness reconnects or expands the field of energy. You will sense or perceive the change. In terms of the client's action, it may look like reframing, joining love with the trauma and judgment, or giving themselves permission to accept the forgiveness that is inherent in the creation of the human form. Simply articulating the hurt can produce forgiveness.

Another way to look at self-forgiveness is that our *givingness* precedes those experiences that block or separate us. A play on words helps here. In for-giveness, we reestablish the giving that existed be-for. We reconnect with the a priori giving. This giving exists in the form of giving to ourselves, our loving, and our virtue, and receiving the giving, loving, or virtue from others.

CLINICAL CHALLENGES

Two challenges that seem to be prevalent in my work are what I call *sophisticated clients* and *transference*. Sophisticated clients know too much. With transference, we believe our projections.

Sophisticated Clients

Some of the most challenging people I've worked with have been therapists. Ironically, their knowledge and work on themselves create a perspective or set of beliefs that blocks them. Often they feel they have solved this or that challenge or healed that problem. Their sophisticated models lead them to believe their understanding is complete. A similar phenomenon sometimes occurs with people who have done a lot of therapeutic or growth work. Sometimes this expresses as: "Since I am Divine and perfect, I have nothing to resolve or change." Lots of luck.

Clarity can be an adversary. Explanation can close the door on the next mystery. The ego is very subtle at this point. Therapists often find refuge in their role as helper. They are safe as the facilitator. Subtly, the core self goes to sleep, becomes numb, or hardens. Vulnerability and resilience are keys for the aged therapists, or self-therapists. These are often the people most likely to have difficulty using self-forgiveness. They take issue with the dynamic of self-judgment. Balance by self-forgiveness is too simplistic. Self-forgiveness is a process itself and not a technique that processes issues. Often the one small act that harvests years of good work is a simple "I forgive myself."

Transference

The implications of transference for the practitioner of energy therapy are far reaching and require continual study. In the conventional sense, transference is a phenomenon of the client seeing the practitioner as someone else, a belief, an ideal, or a fantasy, and then, believing that the projection is real. Counter transference is when the practitioner also believes that the projection of the client is real. Any reaction by the practitioner indicates that some form of counter transference is occurring.

The phenomenon of transference occurs in all human relationship. The more intimate or emotionally charged, the greater will be the likelihood of transference. I like to look at transference as a dramatization of our internal states acting itself out in our shared energy fields. In other words, the circle of our souls creates a context or a stage upon which we project, act out, and dramatize our internal dynamics. As the transference runs its course, we perceptually play out the roles of each other's projections.

Transference is a blessing and a curse. When the dramatized inner state is shadow, we are prone to adversity, hurt, and war. When the dramatized inner state is our soul, even the spiritual worlds shining through us, we are prone to cooperation, healing, and peace. In either case, transference is an important vehicle in the process of transformation.

Transference appears to occur because of the interaction of our soul and ego. The basis of the ego is a product of our dualism, our separation, and the identification with that state. The soul is a product of our experience as a process of God. Our souls are capable of merging with each other and with the energy field of the Creator. Our ego, born of dualism, cannot merge. In an ego state, we are not aware that it is our spirits that are attracted and produce the content of our ego, through our perception, as reality. This perception then defines the phenomenon we respond to as reality. When we are fully awakened in our soul-space, this phenomenon still occurs, but as a peripheral event, not as a defining event.

As practitioners, our noetic field is a mirror for the client's transference and we strive to respond (counter transference) from our soul-space. Counter transference is inevitable. Our soul response draws the client's shadow or negativity (dualism) toward unity. The corrupted soul urge is able to complete itself and become whole either through fulfilling itself or unifying with spirit.

Most blocks are formed by thwarted attempts to actualize a creative urge to share our loving. The use of the pendulum as an instrument of balance in field helps focus the energy of transference into a transformational flow.

As you gain experience as an energy therapist, the spiritual and magnetic power in your consciousness increases. This enhances the transference relationship. Again, this is good news and bad news. When the practitioner is centered, it is good news. When the practitioner feels off center and must compensate to continue working, s/he works harder. The trouble begins when the practitioner is out of center but believes s/he is centered. Clarity and self-assurance are the subtlest of adversaries in this context. You must proceed from an intention to serve the highest good of the client while surrendering any agenda to accomplish anything you believe is good for the client. The simple act of engaging a client as client is a form of counter transference, a projection, an agenda. Hold an alignment and surrender all agendas to the spiritual force field that your alignment made possible.

As you grow in magnetic power and spiritual authority, you can actually convert the client to your own projection and believe that you are acting therapeutically. In a sense, you can build a form into the energy field of the client that is a construct of your prejudice and adapt the client's energy to accept it as its own. There is a fine line between converting someone to a belief about God and converting someone in the sense of assisting them to awaken to God through soul alignment.

ENERGY MANAGEMENT

Consciousness is energy that is aware of itself. We have a conditional awareness of consciousness. It is formed by our human condition. Universal consciousness may appear to us as nothing, then, out of the blue, it moves on itself, and unfolds itself to us. The higher aspects of our own nature function in this same dynamic way. Potentially, this is a seamless web of energy that permeates creation and acts as one unified will. Within that larger unity, there is apparently a will to diversity, which begins with conflict and matures in harmony. As a microcosm, within our personal energy space, we are a seamless, conscious energy acting with purpose. How we use our will determines whether we experience ourselves as one, as peaceful, separate, or conflicted. With will, we choose our experience.

Helpful applications of will for the effective management of energy are:

- Consciousness will move according to how you place your attention. Your energy gathers at your point of focus, which in turn attracts the universe to meet you. When you are adversarial, energies polarize for and against you. When you are in unity, everything is for you, even when it seems against you.
- To balance an aura, first learn to pay attention and relax. This is difficult when we are raised to pay attention and become tense. Learn to relax when you engage. Your relaxation becomes a point of attention. The noetic universe meets you as a point and as a field, identifying itself through image, color, sound, or feeling.
- When you align transcendentally through your higher consciousness, you also engage the universal field of consciousness with the horizon of your energy fields. For this, imagine being in the center of an egg-shaped energy field. You are sustained by the universal energy. God will meet you everywhere.

- You can activate the energy-building characteristics of your noetic field through imagination and prayer. One form of this is the practice of looking at the palms of your hands while you surrender into your center. Breathing love amplifies any energy exercise. Sequentially visualize red, orange, yellow, green, blue, indigo, and violet to integrate and energize your aura and the chakras. Chi-gung practices strengthen the energy in your body.
- Because Noetic Balancing requires the partial merging of the practitioner's and the client's aura, the integrity and skill of the balancing process is essential for the health and well-being of the practitioner and the client. Deceit or covert agendas abdicate the help of Spirit. You need to maintain a strong vibrant aura, impeccable character, and a clear, developed spiritual attunement.
- With each breath breathe spiritual energy through your body and space and saying "I love you" to yourself and your body. When anything disturbs you, take it as an unresolved issue in yourself and forgive yourself. With each breath say "God bless you I love you and peace be still," whether to yourself, others, situations or circumstances.

Process Energy

Energy is neutral. Depending on the approach, you could take on negative energy patterns through your relationships, especially in helping relationships. The hierarchy of you and the client makes you more vulnerable. You then have to clear yourself of toxic energy that you psychically acquired. In severe cases, you will clear the acquired energy through illness. In a sense, you can take on the client's karma instead of assisting them to release it. You can also take on experiences from your clients that they need, thereby disrupting their process or the flow of their destiny. You can inadvertently, through an arrogant sense of good, interfere with lessons and experience that clients need to fulfill their life stream.

I call this energy that we take on from client's *process energy*. In counseling literature, the burn out from this is politely called *compassion fatigue*. We pick it up in the process of working with the client, and we pick up more when we do too much processing of the client's patterns. Noetic Balancing works with the natural flow of the client's energy fields as a means of accomplishing balance, alignment, and transformation. This approach is not a process technique, per se. Noetic Balancing is an activity that assists the client to engage, clarify, and release blockages.

The guidelines for *Student's Mind* for developing a healthy response to *process energy* are:

- We are all expressions of the divine. When you approach a client, respond from the sacredness and appropriateness of how they have constructed their consciousness. Have no agenda or attitude about what the client ought to do or ought to be or how to get there.
- Guide facilitative conversation to clarify judgments and perceptions so that the client's articulation, awareness, reframing, and self-forgiveness can allow the particular energy pattern to balance. Forgive yourself with each client self forgiveness.
- Your only motivation is to serve God. You are assisting the process of God in yourself and in your client. In this way, your action is impersonal.
- Always monitor your sense of yourself as a practitioner. If your role begins to define you, you are cautioned. The only fulfillment is in your service and the fullness of your divine connection with another person. There are many secondary rewards, such as the client's well-being. They are never the goal. Our relationship with God is the primary goal.
- Get plenty of spiritual and physical exercise. You will pick up something from your clients no matter how impeccable you are. Physical exercise pushes residue to the edge of your aura and it burns off. Spiritual exercise strengthens your character and lifts the residue to a higher frequency and transmutes it. Directly willing the process energy to leave or go away may actually embed it more. Attunement with and surrendering to the Holy Spirit or Divine Mother will transmute process energy through grace. Any residue of religious prejudice or judgment in the ego will impede divine help.
- One of my favorites is to take the position that I am responsible for my reality. The client is in my reality; therefore, their issues are a mirror to remind me of what I have not cleared in myself. So I say inside, with the client as a reminder to find the pattern in myself, "I am so sorry (to the energy I have used to create the issue), I love you and I forgive myself."

Clearing

There are many ways to clear our energy. The following protocol is helpful after you have finished a session of any kind, whether therapeutic or a debate with a friend. Rebecca Skeele, a colleague, developed the original form of this protocol for her class in Spiritual Science. Though I do not encourage a mindset that obsesses about "picking stuff up" from others, this technique does provide an easy, systematic way to check, just in case.

Did I pick up anything in the aura balancing?

You will now locate what part of your consciousness is holding this disturbance. Using muscle testing, check each of the following areas. Each time, set the intention for your arm/finger to go weak if you are holding the disturbance in that area. When your arm/finger goes weak, place a check by that area and then visualize a large imaginary "pot" where you will place everything that needs to be cleared. You can do this for yourself, or sometimes you may find that it is helpful to do it with a part. Start by *calling yourself forward into the light.*

I set my arm/finger to go weak if I am carrying the disturbance from the Noetic Field Balancing that I did in:

- My physical body

- My history (commonly referred to as karma):
  This life
  Past life
  My DNA (ancestral)

- Levels of Consciousness:
  Mental
  Emotional (Causal)
  Imaginational (Astral)
  Etheric (Archetypal)
  Soul

Clearing Using Spiritual Assistance

Spiritual Assistance (ask inside for spiritual assistance to lift and clear or resolve all negativity, karma, etc—"the imaginary pot"—in any area that you are holding this opening of negativity, for the highest good of all concerned.)

Technique for using Spiritual Assistance to clear "the imaginary pot' (read silently and hear spoken inwardly):

- Using intention, see or send your consciousness 67 ft (or more) above your head and contact Source (Father/Mother God, All That is, etc.)
- Say inside, "Father/Mother God, it is commanded that the highest light and love come down through all of my levels, into the energy field around my body and into my body to lift, clear and resolve all negativity,

karma, imbalance, judgment, dis-ease, or impinging collateral forces in any area that I am clearing, for my highest good, from these (this) balancing(s), and for the highest good of all concerned.
- It is done, it is done, it is done. (Take a deep breath and release rapidly, then pause and allow Spirit to do the clearing)

Blessing of Completion

Close your eyes and have your partner read out loud or read out loud for yourself. When you read it for yourself, close your eyes after reading until it is complete:

"I ask now for a blessing of light to seal this opening of negativity in my consciousness and in all levels that have been cleared. I ask that this light fill all the places that have been cleared with healing love, truth and grace, for the highest good of all concerned. Amen/So be it"

Chapter Five

NOETIC BALANCING

People from many spiritual backgrounds have come for sessions with me. The differences were never an obstacle. With true spirituality, there is never a conflict. The conflict comes from the dogmatic evolution of a given teaching or teacher. The earth-based *goddess*, the Buddhist *beingness* and quest for *Buddahood*, the Native American *Great Spirit*, the Jewish *Yahweh*, the Taoist *Tao*, the Muslim *Allah*, to name a few, are complementary ways of engaging *universal Holiness*. I am not saying they are the same. I am saying there is no conflict between any true spiritual alignment. Even the mystical Christianity, and awakening the "inner Christ," finds a place with more fundamentalist viewpoints. Within the sacred space created by this divine relationship, wondrous things can happen. Sometimes our expectations are met or surpassed. Other times, nothing appears to happen. That is the way of the Holy Spirit. We always choose to be in our Holiness or in our minds thinking about our Holiness.

Spiritual work is non-adversarial and non-coercive. True spirituality embraces the curriculum of our souls and honors our choices, regardless of how they may seem. Spirit will intervene only at our request. We also appear to be inherently linked to a divine plan or sacred matrix that perpetually prompts us to seek wholeness, fulfillment, peace, loving, joy, and home.

In our ego, we want to do life separate from God. We want the universal to conform to our idea of it. Transformation requires that we choose to do it with God, which is the essence of self-forgiveness. Because we have created a backlog of actions based on separation from self (dualistic mindset), grace may not appear immediately evident in our forgiveness. Within this context, an altered state of consciousness is created that enhances our rapport with others. In this kind of relationship, we are able to communicate through our higher senses. We communicate through the oneness. Angels, spiritual guides, and numerous holy forces may participate in serving and healing through a unified relationship. We are able to discern blocks and may perceive information about the nature, cause, and judgment associated with imbalance. Coaching more and telling less is more efficient, effective, and healthier. In effect, we engage our ego reality and insert an awareness of higher consciousness through resolving our own thoughts of separation.

Noetic Balancing requires us to surrender to the highest spiritual source possible. As I teach this, it is an alignment with the Father-Mother God through the Christ (Jesus Christ if you prefer). Certainly, this is the Christ as a mystical force, a transcendent and present being, and the Holy Spirit. Therefore, it is just as accessible through Allah the Merciful, or for that matter, any deep alignment with Source. In my experience, the deeper the alignment, the greater the results. Noetic Balancing honors any healing or transfomational therapy, physical or otherwise; however, the focus is to utilize all symptoms as a mirror to enhance the soul's agenda to align more deeply with Source, and to reference self-identify to essence. It is out of these actions that all blessings arise. It is a "seek first the Heaven within and all else will be added" approach. As we develop our internal trust with self, the connection to Spirit grows stronger.

Through the years the practice of balancing has evolved. Noetic Balancing, as presented here, is an evolution. However, certain basics concerning the practitioner remain constant and foundational. In the words of Ellavivian Power, this admonition continues to be the foundation for us all (Power, 24-25):

To balance with the Light, one must have some understanding of the Light, and one also must have come through a form of spiritual purification.

At the karmic level, the Aura [Noetic Field] Balancer must have, at some time, faced the karma that he has deposited in these centers; must have faced himself in the situation in which he [she] erred, and must have gone through the process of regeneration. The purer the physical, emotional and spiritual bodies of the Aura [Noetic Field] Balancer, the purer the manifestation of the Light which passes through the pendulum with which he [she] balances the aura of another. Naturally, this being the case, he is always working for a keener insight into himself as well as others. In a sense, he [she] is both a mystic and an adept for he [she] must have, not only a cognizance of the inner planes, but he must at all times be fully aware of all that is taking place on the Earth Plane. He [she], too, must be aware of every word transmitted in the balancing room as well as to know and understand the auric framework that the individual brings to the . . . [session].

. . . He [she] must at all times be able to contact his own soul and work through it. For it is through the soul contact that he [she] can contact the soul

with whom he [she] is working. He [she] is able to do this by contacting his own spiritual will, for it is through this reference that the balancing must be brought into activity.

Preparing the Client

When a client makes an appointment, the practitioner talks about the need to be accepting and that one's own desires for greater health, well-being, and happiness are sufficient preparation. Abstaining from the use of recreational drugs two weeks before and abstaining from moderate alcohol use the day before can also help. If there is drug or alcohol abuse, a longer time of abstinence may be needed. This abstention may not always be possible, so in cases where substances are a concern, the practitioner must decide on a case by case basis. There is great confusion in our culture concerning drugs. There is a widespread belief that we can solve our health and emotional needs by medicating them. Medication has its place, of course. Our concern is that the frequencies communicated by these substances diffuse or compete with the balancing process. When the client's relationship to substances is an issue, that becomes the first priority. Often a substance issue is easily resolved by providing accurate information. In any case, the client needs to understand how their use and attachment to substances affects the alignment, balance and perception of reality. For the first session the client needs to understand the effect of their relationship to substances. For continuing sessions, demonstration in the form of a change in behavior must be evident, or there is no value in continuing. Substances infuse fantasy realities with an aura of truth.

Just as the practitioner must relinquish any agendas for the client, there can be no promises to the client as to the outcome of the work. The balancing process is in service to a deep level of actualization. We are facilitating, with the client, a greater direct participation in spiritual consciousness. This is what we mean by the "highest good." When we accept that the intelligence acting through the balancing contains the soul's will, then we know the "highest good" is mediating the work. Our skill is to follow the lead of those higher levels of knowing, that our alignment with universal, unconditional love make possible. In short, balancing is a spiritual approach, so no promises can be made.

We all have areas of mental and emotional disturbance that we have forgotten. Greater alignment and understanding of our spirituality and purpose is an innate drive. We adapt to our forgotten hurts and judgment. Clients are often surprised at how different they feel after they are balanced. Some things are easy to change. Other areas may need more time or prolonged counseling before we are ready to balance them. Noetic Balancing is an effective complement to any process of physical or psychological healing and can dramatically facilitate that process. Though miracles can happen, this service is not meant to replace needed medical, psychiatric, or other therapeutic treatment. Rather, balancing is meant to cooperate with all activities and forces that are acting for our mutual well being.

So, in a practical sense, we first orient the client to the nature of the balancing. The client reclines, face up, on a massage table or couch. As we stand next to the reclining client, we form a vertical support for transforming their horizontal sojourn through life. The reclining position of the client is relaxing while providing easy access to the field. The physical and emotional balancing is done silently. If a question or observation comes up, the client is encouraged to speak. During the mental-spiritual balancing, focus statements help the client discover and clarify beliefs, and to facilitate self-forgiveness. Jewelry, metal, and shoes might affect the balancing process, so they are removed. When it is the client's first session with me, I have them read and sign a release statement. This statement clarifies the content and scope of the balancing. The statement I use is as follows:

The purpose of this release form is to clarify the nature of the service you are receiving and our agreement with each other. Noetic Balancing is an application of ancient mysteries to modern therapeutic needs. Noetic means spiritual mind. The noetic field is an aura of energy that surrounds the body. This field reflects our physical, emotional, mental, archetypal and spiritual levels. Spiritual centers, called chakras in yoga psychology, integrate this field and the systems of the physical body. These centers correspond with specific psychological structures.

Blocks in the flow of this energy are caused by judgments that you made, or beliefs that you constructed, in response to challenging or traumatic events. Each issue, or block, serves a deeper intentional soul aim to awaken you to a greater sense of center, wisdom, love or power. As our attachment to our limiting beliefs is transformed, we often have spontaneous awareness of the soul's intention. Distortions in the field are also caused by the tension and emotion of everyday living, which usually balance easily without conversation.

My intention is to serve you in a way that you gain the most from your experience. Since it is a spiritual approach, it is non-inflictive. By that, I mean that your choice and highest good are never violated. From your perspective, give yourself the liberty to forgive yourself for limiting and self-judging beliefs, and allow yourself to respond to the experience as it is offered. Because of the spiritual nature of the service, I make no promises as to the results or outcome you may receive. The effects are often subtle and you may not always be aware of changes. On the other hand, you may be aware of intense changes in new ways. You may need time to adjust to the positive changes resulting from your experience. For that reason, I suggest that you do not engage in sexual activity or the use of alcohol for the three days following your session.

In my experience, consciousness altering, recreational drugs work against the nature of the balancing. By recreational, I am not referring to the use of consciousness altering substances administered under the strict guidance and guidelines of some mystery teachings, or to prescription drugs. Whatever the case, I ask that you abstain from non-prescription drug use for three days following our session.

I work from a spiritual alignment that assists you in your spiritual progression and well being. As the session begins, I will use a prayer that aligns me and evokes a spiritual presence that I call the Christ and Holy Spirit. This alignment is never in conflict with any positive spiritual path and will complement your spiritual practices. It is very compatible with Christian, Buddhist, Sufi (Muslim), Jewish, Taoist, Shamanic and Native American ways. If your fundamental spiritual viewpoint causes you to feel discomfort with my approach, this service may not be appropriate for you at this time.

After the opening prayer, I work silently for awhile, using my hand or a pendulum to sense, connect with the field patterns, and focus balancing energy. As we progress, I assist you to frame appropriate self-forgiveness statements. It is your self-forgiveness that allows higher consciousness to balance any distortions in your field. No set of attitudes or beliefs are imposed upon you. Any suggestions made to you are given as options that may assist you in clearing and balancing your energy field. The balancing process will not exceed the limits that are appropriate for you as expressed by your own intuitive determination of the highest good. I make no claims as to the success or outcome of your experience. There is always a possibility that the session will miss your expectations; however, there is the same likelihood that your expectations will be surpassed.

My background prepares me to sense and understand underlying causes of imbalance, to focus spiritual energy and otherwise assist you to use the experience to your greatest benefit. The Source of change is within you. Consequently, I engage your inner wisdom and healing resources and assist you to forgive or reframe judgments you have made against your own spiritual essence. The pendulum used during this process acts as a tool to detect, release and focus energy. It is no more than an extension of the rapport and spiritual alignment that we share in the balancing relationship.

Noetic Balancing is primarily an educational process that touches many levels of your transformational learning. It does not replace the complementary services of counselors, psychologists, psychotherapists, psychiatrists, chiropractors or medical doctors, or any other professional providing services appropriate to your needs. Though I have training and experience as a therapist, I am primarily a spiritual educator, ministering to your transformational needs and the curriculum of your soul.

After your first session, I recommend two additional follow-up sessions no sooner than two weeks apart. Each session builds a foundation for the next. After the first three sessions, scheduling a session every six to twelve months can be helpful. The final criteria is always your intuitive sense for when the next session would be helpful to you.

There are many energy field therapies available. Each has its unique contribution. Regardless of outer similarities, these services may not be the same, because of differences in practitioners, techniques and spiritual Sources. I encourage you to consider each on its own merit and not compare.

I also teach practitioners in this technique. From time to time, I ask graduates of my practitioner program to observe or assist me in a session. This practice can only add to the quality of the balancing. Of course, if you are uncomfortable with their presence, we will honor your wish.

Prayer

With the client relaxing, I begin with a prayer that goes something like this:

Father-Mother God, I just now ask to be surrounded by the light of the Christ and, through the Holy Spirit, I ask for only that which is to the highest good of all concerned, keeping in mind the destinies on the planet. Through the permission of the Christ and the guidance of the Holy Spirit, I also ask that any angels, beings of light, or teachers who wish to be here and assist for the well-being of all concerned also be granted. We ask for this in perfect love and perfect understanding, and we thank you for this time. Thy will be done.

At this point I may have insights into the consciousness of the client. Engaging the Christ as a spiritual form complements all ways of life and teachings that pursue unconditional loving. Regardless of spiritual heritage, the balancing strengthens the client's particular spiritual practice.

The theory and practice that is now Noetic Balancing began from a mystical and metaphysical perspective of Phineus Parkhust Quimby's *Science of the Christ*. From a Muslim, Hindu, Buddhist, Taoist, or indigenous perspective, this may appear as a fundamentally Christian dogma. Of course, this is very far from the truth. There is a powerful negative force in the dogmatic teachings of any religion that cause the adherents to view their alignment as the only right way to talk about and connect to the Divine forces of the universe. All lineages refer into Source; however, all teachings or groups may not actually connect into Source because of distortions that were incorporated into their heritage. Given that one's approach strives to connect to the field of unconditional love, which I am referring to here as the Christ, or Kristos, then the balancing experience will unfold following compatible protocols.

Some students have difficulty with the prayer I use. When the difficulty comes from their established spiritual practice in some lineage that appears different than mine, this is not a problem. We can develop a prayer that expresses a similar vibratory pattern. When the difficulty comes from religious injury or confused spiritual beliefs or concept, we must heal and transform those patterns, regardless of the prayer. Otherwise, I prefer they use this prayer and strive to discover the universal spiritual science expressed through its intonation. As a guideline to developing a congruent prayer, the opening prayer will always contain certain universal elements that translate into any truly spiritual tradition. The prayer includes an:

- invitation for an alignment with and surrender to a higher power,
- admonition of impeccability,
- sanctification of the place,
- dedication to the highest good, and
- expression of gratitude.

Opening and Balancing

After the prayer, I use a crystal pendulum to open the aura at the solar plexus. The pendulum is an instrument of focus. The permission of the client, the alignment with spirit, and my intention form the focus through the pendulum to engage the aura. On contact, the client's basic self and high self respond to open the aura. The pendulum provides a connection for universal consciousness to unfold in the locality of the imbalance or distortion in the energy field. The practitioner's intention selects the nature of the localizing unfolding activity, and the level of the energy field being balanced. The response from higher consciousness and permission of the client's inner guidance determines the content and structure of the activity. The oscillation of the pendulum reflects the unfolding and enfolding geometries that transform the distortion. The pendulum, at this point, reflects a connection of energy, a location, through which the spiritual forces can assist the client and balance the energy. The pendulum does not cause the activity. It is an effect.

As I lower the pendulum into the energy field, I sense the subtle changes. Usually the noetic connection engages the field and begins to open just above the solar plexus. When this occurs, the pendulum gently begins to rotate. When the field is open, the pendulum stops. The *opened aura* means that rapport has been established and spiritual connection has been accomplished. We open the field at the solar plexus because this is the seat of the basic self. Without the agreement of the basic self, nothing else happens. This action creates a high level of rapport.

It also opens an amplified vulnerability and sensitivity. The protective field of the aura is like a "cell membrane" in that it functions as an interface between the levels of the physical, psychic and spiritual environments. The aura has a permeability based on safety, nurture, emotional, mental and spiritual needs. A healthy balanced field is permeable to positive, supportive energies. A distorted and imbalance field will absorb negativity and energy with an affinity to the types of distortions, blocks and imbalances that exist.

Balancing the aura follows in a similar way. The block is discovered and engaged in a manner that facilitates its transformation. The pendulum oscillates when balancing is occurring and stops when it is done. As mentioned before, blocks are an attempt to protect on one level and have been integrated into the sustaining structure of the individual. On another level, transformation serves the intentional aims of our soul development. Therefore, the individual must "authorize" any change to this structure.

Next, I scan the aura with my hand to first increase my attunement and then to find the blocks and distortions. My hands are trained to see and sense. The impressions are processed through my nervous system and brain like any other stimulation. Because I am awake in my subtle body, movement in my energy fields registers in my physical body. Noetic development helps me discern the deeper soul aims and causes related to the block

When I find a block or distortion, I use the pendulum to engage the energy. When the pendulum rotates, it reflects the transformation of energy that is occurring in the aura. I proceed in this manner until all the areas are balanced. A natural guidance leads from one step to the next. Balancing the physical and emotional energy fields is often done silently. I may ask the client what she or he is experiencing or suggest a deep breath. Facilitative talking is always needed in the mental-spiritual balancing because the client needs to discover and clarify his/her beliefs and self-forgiveness.

At some point toward the end, I will have the client turn over so I can check the aura from the back. I continue until the entire aura is smooth and silky. Before I finish, the client is once again face up.

Closing

When the balancing appears to be complete, the client is asked if there is anything else. When nothing more presents itself, the client releases all concerns into higher consciousness. I proceed to close the field with intention and the blessing of the Holy Spirit. I close the aura by making twelve passes over and around the physical body, and, then, closing at the pineal. I open at the basic self and close at the high self. In the *Standard Procedure* that I teach beginning students, seven passes with the pendulum are completed by closing over the solar plexus. In both cases, opening the aura occurs at the solar plexus.

This entire process usually takes from forty-five minutes to one hour, or occasionally longer. A session that lasts one and one half hours is not uncommon. The client's immediate experience may be as subtle as feeling more peaceful or as dramatic as experiencing bliss, greater clarity or transformation. The balancing process continues for three days after the actual session has ended. During this time, the client completes any processing and adapts to any changes. This period of adjustment provides a new baseline upon which the subconscious (basic self) can regulate the psyche. For that reason, it is recommended that the client abstain from alcohol, recreational drug use, and sex for those three days. Alcohol and drugs may disrupt the transformative changes and disperse the new organization of energy. Sexual intimacy is very powerful and, until the changes stabilize, may be confusing on a subtle level. Recreational drugs always act against the balancing process and should not be used when developing a strong, aligned, balanced aura.

It is recommend that clients take life as it comes for the following three days, and not analyze or worry about their experience. Journaling and reflective insights are often helpful. Changes are often deep and can be accompanied by uncomfortable symptoms such as minor flu or restlessness. On the other hand, the client may experience a great peace or joy. In any case, by the end of the three days, the client will have adjusted to the changes and have a new sense of what is normal. With each session, the client becomes more and more skillful in using the balancing session and maintaining and promoting balance in general. Each session provides a stronger platform for the next session. For that reason, three initial sessions are recommended. These sessions should be at least two weeks apart; however, a longer spacing is fine. After the first three sessions, a touch-up every six to twelve months is recommended. (Practitioners of this technique can be found on the web-site: *www.noeticbalancing.com.*)

FOUNDATION SKILLS

Because of the subtle nature of Noetic Balancing, we need a baseline from which to reference what we are doing. I call this baseline, *foundation skills*, because, by establishing a solid foundation, our practice will develop in a sound way. As part of *foundation*, the Noetic Balancing student has, to this point, studied the prerequisite reading: *Foot Prints of Eternity*. *Foundation* begins with impeccable alignment and radical witness.

Pendulum

The pendulum has a simple and important function in this balancing process. As a focus of energy, it provides a discipline for *Student's Mind*. The activity of the pendulum reflects energy events in the field. Your intention selects the level, dimension or aspect of the field with which you want to form a nexus. For this form of engaging the field to work well, we need to develop an internal discipline so that our own desire or prejudice is filtered from the information stream of the connection. Often this requires us to forgive ourselves for the same block or issue that arises for the client. The pendulum will follow whatever pattern is in your imagination, so you must practice neutrality and have specific agreements with your basic self. The basic self needs an agreed upon protocol in order to respond in an accurate way to our intention. We train our mind to use the convention as a means of giving spirit a conduit or channel through which it can work.

In general, a pendulum is any weighted object on the end of a chain or string. Gravity holds a still pendulum approximately perpendicular to the earth's surface. For balancing work, I prefer a crystal or shaped glass attached to a comfortable length of chain. To begin, hold the pendulum by the chain draped over you index finger. With practice, you will find that the spin will conform to the pattern you are imagining. Imagining clockwise and counter clockwise spins provides a way to test your basic alignment. The purpose of making it spin is so that we can master the choices that allow the pendulum to rotate in response to the pattern in the field and the direction of Spirit. I have students practice finding a block in the aura, and engage it with the pendulum. Depending on how you focus, the pendulum may swing clockwise or counterclockwise. In the beginning, practice a focus that produces a clockwise spin. The energy comes into our psyche from above on a clockwise spiral. The energy below comes into our psyche on a counterclockwise spiral. If your attention wanders, the spin may change. However, if you are paying attention and the spin changes, trust the counterclockwise spin. In your *Student's Mind*, you are always learning. One of the reasons I call this practice Noetic Balancing because a higher consciousness is always working with you through the direction of the Christ (*living love*). So, in your conscious relationship, the pendulum may spin either way. The *living love* of Source disperses the distortions and miasmas in the energy fields. This energy spirals in through a clockwise vortex.

When the pendulum changes it spin or you need clarification, you can use your pendulum to reflect an answer. Continuing from the previous discussion, you establish a convention. The one I use is that a clockwise spin means "yes" and a counterclockwise spin means "no." Hold the pendulum in one hand, usually your right, over the index knuckle of the other hand. Mentally ask your question in a way that can be answered yes or no. This technique provides you with an added way to reflect on highly subjective events.

In all cases you are exploring the reality of the client in particular and the reality of multidimensional consciousness in general. Your alignment with Holiness is the only gauge of truth. So, regardless of what the pendulum is doing, you continually check inwardly with Source.

Finding and Balancing Blocks

Generally, we scan with our hand to find distortions and blockages in the aura. The sensation varies. As we attune to the disturbed energy pattern, and deconstruct our preconception, while placing our focus on our inner screen, images appear that reflect the energy pattern to which we are attuning. The images on the inner screen guide our dialogue with the client.

Focus Statements

In the mental/spiritual level of the balancing, tracking the self judgements and the limiting beliefs of each block is an art in and of itself. Focus statements assist the client to access precise information based on each block. Each structure has a morphogenetic field that interpenetrates the other. Change in one affects change in the other. Each chakra has a functional relationship to the whole consciousness. The chakras are a major interface between the geometric structure of the multidimensional aspects of self and the subtle elements of the physical body. Each chakra relates to a specific psychological dynamic. By referring to the chart in the next section, Standard Procedure, you can see the areas of constellated beliefs that correspond to each chakra. The numbers in the chart indicate the sequence you follow. Beginning at the solar plexus, you say: "Tell me about a time when you were afraid, powerless, abandoned or alone." The client responds. You then work with them to develop forgiveness statements, which they, then, state out loud. The Light clears and transforms the block with each self-forgiveness.

Client Themes

Through your witness and engaging the energy block through touch, or with the pendulum, you create a conduit for universal love and a presence of the Holy Spirit to reconfigure the field miasmas that we are calling energy blocks. By facilitating the deconstruction of the block the soul force can reconfigure the pattern. Blocks become stepping stones through this process. The focus of *Light* through the pendulum also creates a vortex though which forms can manifest and de-manifest from one dimension to the next. What this means is that the nonlocal cause can reconfigure the space directly from the causal reality.

As you work through each block, a pattern emerges that reveals the *destiny themes* of the client. The *destiny themes* are intentional forces that the soul wants to actualize. These may have to do with unresolved karmic issues or new areas of growth and development. The destiny themes serve as a mechanism by which the individual selects the situations and circumstances that comprise experience. By deconstructing the block, the miasmas are dissolved and actualization promoted.

The sequence of work proceeds through the physical, emotional and mental/spiritual levels. The physical level relates to health and the wear and tear of living life physically. There are emotional and mental patterns that manifest physically. Stress, attitude and beliefs do result in physical imbalance and illness. Those issues are dealt with on the level that is causing them.

You use your feeling, sensation and awareness skills selectively to feel blocks in the field. You select with you mind: I am feeling only blocks in the physical aura. You are able to select in this way. You are discovering the moment and learning the discrete configuration in the energy. You then engage that configuration through the pendulum or touch. Your alignment makes the balancing automatic. The pendulum oscillates until the miasma clears.

Developing your style of Noetic Balancing evolves from your innate potential. Style, skill and technique have several levels. One level has to do with the centrality to your own destiny. Is it a catalyst to something else you need to fulfill or a major element of your fulfillment? If you are a counselor or a healer is it supplemental, or your featured service? These questions answer themselves as you develop experience and mastery.

When developing the art and skill of Noetic Balancing, pay attention to the interplay between action and reflection. Life has a cause and effect, a karma, a dharma. You are inherently mandated to become a responsible creator. When it is not in the flow of your destiny to practice Noetic Balancing, you are not as well equipped to handle the consequences. Not to fear. In any case, you can learn to master the "compassion fatigue" or residual energies you might have to process due to your transformational facilitation. Again, we must each become aware of our own style and nature when opening to this application of our noetic nature.

Like physical geography, you find your way through the aura and noetic dimensions by establishing reference points. Some are natural, and some you must construct. As you develop a working foundation in practical understanding and skill, keep in mind the fine line between *what you create* to facilitate and the *actual reality* of consciousness. In a sense, you create the client so you can heal yourself.

No matter how effective, your methods of discovery and application are projections based on your level of understanding. Methodology is a form of counter-transference. This is one reason why you must always facilitate the progress inherently prescribed in the nature and history of the client as a sacred entity. The unfolding Holiness of the client is the guide. Keep this admonition in mind. Always be vigilant. The tendency is to define yourself and the client on the basis of your clarity, knowledge, and skill. You can never avoid this one hundred percent, but you can practice the awareness that in your mastery you dance on the edge of truth and fiction.

Procedure and style guide your actions. They are pragmatic and necessary forces that enable effective results. Confidence must always be in your sense of soul. When you are firmly anchored in spirit, your action will follow with the effect of spirit. Your own style of working will emerge as a form of mentoring from your soul. These procedures will form a foundation and baseline from which you will continue to evolve, deepen, and refine your skill. Remember, consciousness is the foundation. It establishes the context, perceptive selection, and unfolding procedure. There are five procedural styles, which I call *Standard, Drawing Out, Functional, Developmental,* and *Archetypal.*

Once you gain confidence by practicing the Standard Procedure, you will inevitably find your own style emerging. You may always feel the standard works best for you. It always works when nothing else presents itself, and it is the foundation upon which you develop your style. In all cases check your work.

STANDARD PROCEDURE

Standard Procedure is also a foundation or base line protocol. The approach in this section will teach an important discipline as a guide to understanding. Once this standard is internalized, experience will continue to teach and refine your ability and consciousness. This procedure will help you establish a strong base of experience and understanding in the structure, practice, and process of Noetic Balancing. The process also provides an opportunity to review and transform sources of glamour or rebellion that may be driving or confusing your sense of style. The more you develop, the subtler the obstacles. The favorite refuge for rebellion and glamour resides in our clarity and sense of calling or mission.

Orientation

The Standard Procedure provides a baseline, a reference from which to proceed and guide your progress. It is like the "You are here" sign on a map that orients us. It is the basic format from which the other procedures continue, so follow it strictly until experience tells you it is time to expand or modify your approach. The format of the Standard Procedure is the same for all the approaches. The part that changes is in how you formulate your questions.

Begin all levels of balancing by taking a moment to focus on your intent and to engage higher consciousness. State the prayer, connect with the client's field at the solar plexus, and initiate rapport through opening the aura. Once this is accomplished, scan the aura with your hand. This familiarizes you with the energy patterns and reveals the areas of congestion, and heightens your noetic sensitivity. Begin at the solar plexus, then the feet, and then progress up the body. The solar plexus is the center of our body-based reality, and the feet are our foundation on the earth. Depending on the circumstances or client's need, the physical, emotional, and mental-spiritual balancings can be performed as separate sessions or phases of the same session.

First Session or Phase. You say to the client that the physical and emotional balancing is primarily silent (except perhaps to help the client relax and let go). Sometimes, however, patterns in the physical and emotional energy fields extend into the mental energy field. In those cases, you may dialogue to draw the client out. In the physical and emotional stages, proceed to balance the field at each focus area, following the numbered sequence on the following diagram: 1. Open; 2. Solar Plexus; 3. Below Feet and Legs; 4. Sacral and Root; 5. Heart; 6. Throat; 7. Face and Head; 8. Above Top of Head (following central axis); 9. Back (client turns over); 10. (Client turns over) Approximately 12" above head; 11. Approximately 12" below bottom of feet (on central axis); 12. Close (solar plexus or pineal, making seven or twelve passes with pendulum over and around the client.)

The physical balancing focuses on the physical and etheric fields. It is often helpful to ask if there has been any serious injury or illness. Check those areas and continue to move through the aura. Starting at the solar plexus, engage each block with the pendulum. A flow of energy may or may not be evident. When the oscillation of the pendulum stops, proceed to the next area of attention. From time to time, you may ask the client to take a deep breath to facilitate the release.

Second Session or Phase. When the emotional balancing is a separate session from the physical, begin by checking the physical aura. The emotional balancing focuses primarily on the emotional field. You may actually feel the emotional content of the block. Proceed as you did in the physical balancing, except focus on the emotional level. From time to time, you may assist the client by asking what s/he is experiencing.

Third Session or Phase. This balancing clarifies and forgives beliefs and judgments against oneself. The mental-spiritual balancing focuses in the mental, causal, archetypal, and soul levels. When the mental-spiritual balancing is a separate session from the physical and emotional balancings, check the previous sessions again. This checking proceeds by passing your hand, or your awareness, through the field to detect any blocks or distortions. If you find any you then balance them, and proceed to the next step.

During the mental-spiritual balancing, you say to the client that you are going to make some focus statements (see the following diagram). As the client reflects on these statements, you want the client to share whatever occurs. The reflection provides a focus for the unconscious. The client's response will appear as an image, insight, feeling, or other recall. The focus statements are made in the same sequence as the silent balancing.

Each dialogue focus statement corresponds to the number indicated on the following diagram:

1. Open field.
2. Tell me about a time when you were alone, afraid, abandoned, or hurt or experienced guilt or shame.
3. Tell me about a time when you were confused or didn't understand, felt unsupported, or had no place or didn't belong.
4. Tell me about a time when you judged your sexuality or creativity, or had resentment.
5. Tell me about a time when you had regret, felt disappointed or betrayed, or tried to share your loving and couldn't with others or yourself.
6. Tell me about a time when you experienced difficulty speaking, or because you spoke.
7. Tell me about a time when you saw or heard something that was painful, disturbing, or frightening.
8. Tell me about a time when you wanted revenge, to get even, prove yourself by a standard.
9. Usually silent. Burdens, betrayals, or anger may appear.
10. Usually silent. Spiritual alignment.
11. Usually silent. Spiritual alignment
12. Close field. (Pass over and around the body twelve times, then lower pendulum over solar plexus or pineal.)

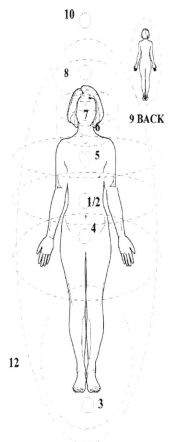

You may also ask about an age or image that appears to you. You might feel an emotional state such as confusion or sadness and ask the client to elaborate. For example, I trusted an inner impression and asked a client, "Does a red fire truck mean anything to you?" After a moment, he said, emotionally, "It was the only one I could talk to." He was a very sensitive child and felt isolated in his early childhood. His red fire truck was his only safe, reliable companion.

The balancing occurs through awareness, reframing, and forgiveness. This level includes verbal clarification as needed. Less is better. Always work at your own comfort level. Choose comfort with impeccability.

Some guidelines for assisting the client are:

- Clarify if the incident was the result of commission or omission. In other words, did the incident happen because the client did something, or because they failed to do something?
- Clarify the client's judgments against self by exploring shame, blame, guilt, inferiority, powerlessness, inadequacy, shoulds or oughts.
- Guide the client to reframe, bring to awareness, or clarify self-forgiveness. The self-forgiveness is spoken aloud. After forgiving, have the client take a deep breath and exhale. Often, the breath itself will release the block.
- Self-forgiveness is specific. "I forgive myself for believing that I was _____ because of what happened." There are many variations to this. Sometimes there is a tendency to forgive oneself for "thinking" or "feeling." This is rarely appropriate. Thinking and feeling are processes of information. *Beliefs* are psychological formulae that structure our consciousness, and blind us to the judgment.
- Always assume that the block in the client has a counterpart in you, and forgive yourself inwardly and silently just before you ask the client to do so. This action on your part creates a reality field which facilitates the client's transformation.

Each area of the back corresponds to the area of focus on the front, with slight changes in perspective. The lower back often holds anger or resentment. The heart area might be more sentimental or the client may be carrying another as a burden. Shoulders often incorporate taking responsibility for what one sees, hears, or feels in the actions of others. You do not have to attend to each center on the back as specifically as the front, and you may find that you can talk less or not at all. When you complete the back, you return to the front. Check all the levels and ask if the client is aware of anything else.

When all is done and the aura is smooth and silky, ask the client to breath and release everything or to place everything into the Light. Close the aura. To close the aura, begin at the solar plexus. I usually rotate the pendulum clockwise while visualizing light or spiritual energy filling the aura. Circle the rotating pendulum clockwise around the client seven or twelve times, depending on your prompting. Be sure to encompass the entire body. Then, about a foot from the solar plexus, or pineal, lower the pendulum with the intention to close the aura. When the pendulum stops rotating the aura is generally closed. Through your high-self alignment, check with the client's basic- and high-self to see if the balancing and closing is complete. If not, use a figure eight pattern, or hold your focus until the pendulum indicates the closing is complete.

MERIDIANS

The meridians are conduits of energy that flow up and down the body, transporting energy along the etheric sheath that is about three to twelve inches from the physical body. These channels of energy are also called *axional lines*. These channels feed vitality to the subtle body, etheric double and the meridians. Normally, there is a strong central channel and five lines on each side. Actually there are six, counting the flow from a point just above the top of the head around the periphery of the body into the center just below the feet. This meridian usually activates when the others are balanced completely. You can test the flow of this energy by holding the pendulum over the fingers, thumbs or toes. The energy will show as an oscillation in the pendulum, either circular or back and forth. When the energy is not flowing, we are cut off from the cosmic Source of energy, and pull energy from our organs. If we over-use our organs, they become depleted and wither away, causing death.

Ellavivian Power was one of the early pioneers of aura balancing in its modern form. She was one of my mentors. She wrote the definitive book on balancing, the *Auric Mirror*. In the section on Etheric Attunement she state: "The purpose of the Etheric Attunement is two-fold. It is formulated as a protection against any kind of psychic attack and entity possession and to give an added impetus to the achievement of a definite goal or purpose." (Powers, 36) In oriental medicine, the practitioner adjusts points of energy along meridian lines in order to effect balance and restore health. Though the specific map for the meridian lines is different in acupuncture and the map shown here, there is a correspondence. These channels of energy are also called *axiotonal lines*. In the subtle body around the physical body complementary channels of energy feed energy through the meridians.

The meridians become broken, or out of phase, when our actions in the world are not congruent with our spiritual purpose, disrupting the flow of energy through our body. When our actions are congruent, fulfilling soul intentions, then the meridians connect to the cosmic flow of energy. "If we are spiritually motivated in all that we do, we align ourselves with the universal flow of energy; but if we are materially minded and collecting material wealth is our sole motivating power, we cut ourselves off from the Source of all energy." (Powers, 38)

When these lines are weakened or broken, we are vulnerable to the material or forces in the psychic field around us. We gather to us forces that complement our motivation. When our motivation is entirely material, we attract denser energy and become obsessive. When our material goals are congruent with the spirit, our worldly accomplishment serves a greater purpose for the planet or humanity in some way. In this sense, all vocations are of a higher nature, depending on whom or what we serve. For this reason, it is important for us to have work that we love and that is expansive for us. Work done from fear, obligation or because we should, can weaken our energy flow.

If the central meridian is broken, one has probably gone against their nature altogether and is cut off from Source because of a direct opposition to their Devine nature. In some cases the anti self motivation is so strong that the current is reversed or locked. In these cases the individual will die, or become powerful through highly predatory behavior in material and occult ways. This can also appear as a normal flow of energy up though higher levels to a degree. In such cases there is a lesser "Source" for the magnetic flow of energy that has a quality of higher power to it, but is accessing an imaginal (fantasy), emotional (addictive), mental (imposter thought form) or archetypal (demi-god) substitute. This is rare.

Balancing

Powers' approach to repairing the meridian lines uses a pendulum with the intent of repairing the flows of energy. "In order for a person to operate at his [or her] spiritual, intellectual and physical energy peak, the energy should flow up and down these meridians unimpeded and uninterrupted." (36) When we are congruent in our action and soul intent these lines are healthy and vibrant and fold us into the universal flow of energy through creation.

When using a pendulum to balance, the practitioner makes six passes down the body from head to toe and six passes up the body from toe to head, about 12 inches from the physical body. When passing down the body the pendulum will swing counter clockwise and when passing up the body the pendulum will swing clockwise. When you encounter a break or area of congestion, the pendulum will swing from side to side. When the given area is repaired, the pendulum will resume its respective clockwise or counter clockwise swing, depending on whether one is going up or down the body. You continue systematically through all twelve passes. When completed, the flow will once again be congruent.

During this process, the client may become aware of patterns, tendencies, habits or instances when actions were incongruent with his or her deeper soul purposes. When this occurs, self forgiveness can facilitate the repair. The attunement can also be performed in support of an action. In this case the client focuses on the intention/action to be completed while the attunement process is done. If the intention/action is in conflict, it will reflect in the meridian. When a block or break will not resolve in this approach, you can assist the client to discover wherein lies the conflict. This may require a reevaluation of one's motives. When the conflict is resolved, the meridian will repair.

When using just the hand to balance, the practitioner can also repair the meridians through open hand touch. When the practitioner has the sensitivity, a pass with the hand and intention to align the meridians works well. The practitioner passes six times down and six up as in the pendulum technique. An electrical sensation will occur in the palms of the hand. When you encounter a break, you will feel a static discharge, break, or a drag in the energy. Repair occurs by a gentle hand movement up and down the meridian with an intent to repair. A definite flow will occur when the repair is accomplished. When a practitioner is not available, you can also repair or vitalize the meridians by lying flat on your back and visualizing energy flowing into the meridians, coming in through your hands and feet.

Chapter Six

DEVELOPING STYLE

As you develop your balancing skills, you must allow your inner wisdom to shape your style. For some, it may be best to do only physical balancing and avoid facilitating the client's self-forgiveness. If you are going to facilitate self-forgiveness, develop a clear way of doing so. You must practice the procedures and discover your style while remaining true to the precepts of Noetic Balancing. For example, if you change the technique, you are in a different karmic flow than if you neutrally follow the guidelines. Some of us must innovate and some of us must be methodical. This is the rub, so to speak. Is your ego leading you by the subtle end of your nose or is the soul moving you toward an appropriate new horizon?

Ultimately, it doesn't matter because any course leads to course correction. The guideline is to always test, proceed slowly, study the consequence, and modify whatever aspect of yourself, your approach, or your understanding is necessary. Remember, your goal is not to balance someone's aura. Your goal is to awaken in the heart of the divine. Assisting others is one of those skillful means, so your intention is to give the client your best in keeping with their highest good, while being present as a witness. In this way there is no vicarious need fulfillment on your part, and you are in the highest cooperation with the Holiness that is doing the work. Further, you can regard the client as a mirror for areas or issues that are unresolved in yourself. By assuming responsibility in this way, your own self forgiveness clears you, as well as the client, and that type of issue in the collective.

In all cases, check your work. You can check by using your clairvoyance, intuition, and inner seeing, or by using a pendulum technique. I encourage my students to be proficient using the pendulum technique in addition to whatever else they do. It serves as a means of enquiry, learning and verification.

When I check to see if the aura is closed, a counter-clockwise rotation indicates that it is not closed. Generally the aura closes during the action of filling it with light at the end of the session. When more closing is needed, I pass my hand in a figure eight pattern over the client, crossing at the solar plexus. Generally I move my hand in a counter-clockwise approach. I may ask how many passes would be good. I do this by counting while watching the rotation of the pendulum. The rotation will change to a clockwise spin at the right number.

At times, I use this technique to check internal information related to the client. Using this technique requires vigilance and impeccability. It is possible to make the pendulum rotate anyway we want. We can also create convincing perceptions to support any preconception we want to foster, as if what we see is real. This technique is not immune to our biasing tendencies, beliefs, or counter transference. Discipline and integrity form our perennial guides.

Regardless of variation, approach or style, any balancing will include the same three steps.

- First session or phase, silently follow the sequence on the chart, balancing the physical level of the aura.
- Second session or phase, silently follow the sequence on the chart, balancing the emotional level of the aura.
- Third session or phase, prompting reflection and self-forgiveness with each step, following the steps of the chart and balance the mental-spiritual level of the aura.

When I learned aura balancing, we did separate physical, emotional, and mental-spiritual balancings. When time and circumstances did not permit, we often combined the three levels into one session. The sequence does not change. When the physical need is great, even though the balancings are combined, the session may be predominately physical.

Normally, the first three balancing sessions are at least two weeks apart. There can be a longer time between balancing sessions. Two weeks are a minimum. When this sequence is followed, it may be appropriate to venture into the emotional and mental levels in the first session. The client may be ready to move forward, or the physical block may have emotional and mental components. Within the protocol is variation.

Your readiness also determines the nature of the work. It is best to be conservative. Doing just a physical or silent balancing is very powerful. Your intention sets the level of work. Silent work can proceed through all the levels and be effective for the client.

After the first three sessions, regardless of conventions, further balancings continue to be supportive to the client. The followup sessions are usually from six months to a year apart. When spaced closer than six months, there is often little to do.

The goal is always to facilitate, not to process. Processing in an aura balancing impedes the client's progress and causes you to take on unnecessary released energy from the client. A need to process may indicate counter-transference on your part, and indicate that you need to do more inner work as a complement to working with others. As much as possible, you must walk a fine line of impeccability. Ideally, you are invisibly "midwifing" the unfolding love within the client. Your intention is to act through serving the flow of the Creator. As you grow in skill and experience, greater refinement and sophistication will be given to you. Each time you work with a client or yourself, you are taught and guided through spirit. It is through your inner spiritual form, and its mystical union, that you do the work.

The following are examples of balancing styles: *Drawing out, Functional, Developmental,* and *Archetypal.*

DRAWING OUT

The root term for education is "educaré," which means to draw forth. To teach from a transformational learning perspective means to draw forth from the student's inner resources, called the *inner teacher.* This process transforms the student. The same dynamic occurs whether the learning is behavioral, affective, cognitive, or transpersonal. Subject matter is a means, not an end. The goal of transformational learning is the actualization of the soul's curriculum.

Skill

You will be developing intuition, higher sense perception (HSP), and communication skills. Though the pattern follows the same sequence as the Standard Procedure, the style may be more intuitive in that through your inner senses you are perceiving information that you formulate into a focus statement with the intent to draw the rest of the story from the client. Once the story appears, your goal is to direct your questioning in a manner that helps the client discover the pertinent self-judgments and then to frame the self-forgiveness effectively. The function is similar to that of the Standard Procedure. It provides a focus for the client's reflection and response. It is in the reflection that the client engages the flow of his/her *inner therapist.* Develop this procedure gradually, elaborating on the example of the Standard Procedure.

Concept

Images may appear showing great clarity and detail. These images may be exact information intuited from the client's experience. The subtlest pressure on the client's flow of consciousness remains crucial. So, you are encouraged to phrase fact as question rather than statement. Sometimes images are symbolic. In any case, if the information is treated as metaphor, the truth is enhanced without distracting the client over the validity of the images. The client's response will clarify the truth and validate those facts that are helpful.

Process

While you work with the energy fields, encourage the client to speak about whatever concern, feeling, or awareness is present. If the block doesn't clear, ask the client to say more. Through your empathetic relationship, you may experience the client's emotion or perceive an image. Ask, "Could you tell me about _____?" or "I see (or feel) _____. Could you tell me about that?" or "Is there any way you diminish yourself or contract?" or ask, "Is there any way that you are making yourself wrong or less?" The goal is to discover self judgment. If none is evident, have the client forgive self for judging self for what happened.

FUNCTIONAL

Subject content is an element of process. The sequence of prompts in the Standard Procedure expands into a sensitivity to the structural and functional terrain that constitutes our psyche. Just as we live in a greater environmental ecology, there is an ecology within us. The external metaphors become internalized in an orderly and precise way based on our structural-functional nature. This procedure develops your skill to preserve, discern, evaluate, and respond to the client.

Skill

Prompting, drawing out, and clarifying are always part of the dialogue with the client. A functional understanding of the centers of consciousness and chakras provides greater flexibility and deepens your ability to guide the client. In some ways, this is an aesthetic skill. Sensitivity to form and structure refines our awareness of balance, alignment, and the forces acting upon those functions. This procedure also trains your mind and perception to discern universal relationship within the human psyche.

Concept

Each chakra is a center of consciousness and represents the needs and expressions of our lives. Each center is distinct and functions in relationship with all the other chakras. The chakras are mediating centers between the nerve plexus and endocrine system and the psychic, psychological, and spiritual structures. These centers form an etheric anatomy distributing spiritual energy into the various aspects of our lives.

Process

We give parts of ourselves away to what we consider to be important. As we do this, that external power dominates the related psychological structure-function. For example, our culture requires us to give away parts of ourselves in order to conform to role expectations. We give important parts of ourselves away in relationships. In severe cases, a crisis in identity ensues because substantial portions of one's essence are trapped and unable to mature.

Because aspects of ourselves are splintered off from our center, we continue to compensate for our lacks through others. In these relationships, the network of dispossessed soul-essence may be complex. In Huna, the connections are seen as actual energy conduits called "aka chords."

We may give our sexuality to our partner based on family beliefs or familiar roles. We may give our body image away to a cultural standard. Any way we define our worth, value, or integrity in terms of extrinsic social standards may require us to retrieve our essence or life force. To create balance and alignment, we forgive ourselves for defining our value, worth, or integrity extrinsically in terms of family or cultural beliefs, and reclaim the life force that was bound in that way. We abandon part of ourselves to other people literally, symbolically, and metaphorically. For actualization to occur, some form of soul-essence retrieval may be necessary. The energy of our aura is bound into the split-off patterns. As we reclaim and reintegrate these energies, the balance of the aura is enhanced. Often, we can simply breathe these split off or disowned aspects of self into ourselves by visualizing the aspect as an image of self, slowly inhaling, and seeing that aspect return through the top of our head into our physical body (see Re-Placing protocol, Chapter 7).

DEVELOPMENTAL

From conception on, our biological development creates a greater presence in the world. Each developmental cycle combines three elements: the biology itself, the relationship of the organism to the environment, and the capacity of the physical body to hold the energy of the increasingly powerful aspect of our Soul. Depending on external conditions and internal resilience, positive or negative energies are incorporated into our somatic nature. Between conception and birth, these cycles are in trimesters. At physical birth, these cycles are seven years in length. For a detailed understanding of these cycles, review the material in Chapter Four, Journey of the Soul, in *Foot Prints of Eternity* (Waterman, 2006), as you explore the developmental approach.

Skill

The developmental procedure strengthens your ability to travel through the life span with the client, view life as the curriculum of the soul's journey, and see the embedded life span in the metaphor of a given issue or situation. It develops the ability to:

- be sensitive to the life span as a soul agenda for lifelong learning,
- perceive the developmental stages as the context of the various aspects of a soul's nature, and
- discern the personal-social relationship as metaphor and allegory.

These are essential skills for the maturing practitioner. Life themes provide helpful keys for unlocking limiting structures. The Time Angel protocol (Chapter 7), is an example of a developmental technique.

Concept

This procedure incorporates an understanding of the way beliefs are formed across the life span. Contemplation of the material on Piaget, Erickson, Pearce, Steiner, and passages of the Soul, in *Foot Prints of Eternity,* Chapter Four, will help you organize your experience and access intuitive understanding.

Steiner believed that at conception a time line begins through which our organic development and our basic self joins with our psychic and spiritual bodies. As each biological stage matures, it is a harmonious receptacle for the related subtle body. When stages are forced, imbalance occurs. When circumstances are antagonistic or not supportive to the creative aspect of a cycle, we attempt to integrate conflicting forces into our psychobiological structure. We adapt inadvertently to destructive and degenerative forces. This perspective is at the heart of Steiner's view of education and Erickson's life stages.

Process

Techniques in this procedure all involve some form of using the time line or developmental cycles to identify and heal the beliefs or judgments related to traumatic events. Essentially, these techniques either bring the past event to the present, or involve journeying to the past. Many techniques exist for both. Like any approach, our intelligence only needs a focus and it will retrieve or guide us to whatever is needed. Erickson's stages provide a matrix for developmental healing. Issues with doubt, guilt, and trust can be used to bracket an earlier age in which the traumatic event occurred or the developmental age of a recalled event can indicate the characteristics of the issue. Erickson's developmental stages parallel Steiner's beliefs and provide excellent guidance for balancing.

Pearce believes there are two more important steps in the teenage years. At 13 and 16, he believes a spiritual window opens that invites the individual to engage in a connection with higher consciousness, to engage an infinite, divine sense of oneself. If the individual is not met or engaged in this impulse, the drive may express negatively. Negative forms may express as body disfigurement, sadomasochism, risking one's life, suicide, drive-by shootings, or drug abuse. These activities express encounters with life and death in which ritual activity and psychic adventures contrast to encounters with the infinite or divine worlds, initiation into higher consciousness, and exploration of and access to inner spiritual realms. From Steiner's perspective, each seven-year stage carries the archetypal potential for progressive initiation, each one building upon the next. The balancing experience carries the potential to recapitulate missed, partial, and distorted initiatory steps.

ARCHETYPAL

The archetypal procedure is, in many ways, a continuation of the developmental procedure. Both focus on the actualization. The developmental emphasis is on how the archetypal forces are unfolding through the developmental experiences. In a sense, the deep movement in our lives is toward creativity, fulfillment, accomplishment, and transformation, and is due to the archetypal action of our soul's intentionality. The conflict arises as these forces express through our ego. The resolution of karma is such an expression. The archetypal forces arise within us and from the episodic context of our lives. It is a "prepare a place and it will come" approach.

The movie, *Field of Dreams,* provides a wonderful metaphor of this phenomenon. It portrays reconciliation on a time line by creating a space in which an archetypal adjustment in the continuum could occur. The protagonist hears a voice in his cornfield, "Build it and they will come." He intuits the message to mean that, if he builds a baseball field, the players will come. He builds it, and famous baseball players who had died appear in his field to complete unfinished business. Paying spectators responded to a mysterious "call," driving from great distances to the converted corn field. They came to witness and fulfill their own dreams and connection to heart, symbolized through the nostalgia of baseball. The protagonist and his own father reunite to complete unfinished business for both of them. When the time line becomes a present phenomenon, we are fully in the archetypal framework. "I am the Alpha and the Omega."

Just as the archetypal framework provides the matrix for the incarnation, it also provides the pattern for the developmental experience throughout the life span. Events provide an archetypal context for experience and relate metaphorically and symbolically to the lifespan archetypes. In a similar way the progress of the balancing builds and energizes a context for deeper levels to emerge. The form and protocol of the balancing itself is an archetype. The unfolding intelligence that guides the balancing presents the archetypal process through the metaphor of our "issues." The archetypal level is generally attended to last in the balancing session.

Skill

The archetypal level challenges you to stay centered and sustain a focus in the absence of accustomed reference points. In place of having awareness, you simply are aware. The archetypal realm is the "face of the deep." You learn how to pursue the substance of nothing and to wait until something emerges. The images you learn to read on this level portray the incarnation of destiny. This level may be inactive in one session and the cornerstone of the next. At this level, there is a subtle upward current. Beyond the "face of the deep" is the "face of God." The archetypal level is like touching the hem of a holy garment.

As the balancing proceeds the metaphor of each issue or each block that is balanced emerges as a thematic continuity. In some conventions this continuity is a karmic theme, or the karmic flow of the lifetime. As the archetypal wisdom of our life passages and initiation becomes apparent, the karmic flow is understood as grace. New challenges are increasingly experienced as grace. As the archetypal level becomes more visible, the relationship between the issues and blocks and the archetype or intentionality that is being fulfilled becomes more evident. Various people have classified these archetypes. Pearson (1991) in *Awakening the Hero Within* lists the twelve archetypes of our journey and their addictive challenges. The addictive challenges are the stepping stones to awakening the archetypal quality as a soul force. Her archetypes of the soul's journey are: *innocent, orphan, warrior, caregiver, seeker, destroyer, lover, creator, ruler, magician, sage,* and *fool*. The archetypes are helpful as metaphors in our life story. These vignettes reflect the actualization of the archetypes as soul aims.

I attended a conference in which Caroline Myss explored the role of archetypes as seed wisdom that we integrate into our character through life's lessons. Her four archetypes are: *victim, prostitute, saboteur,* and *child*. In this case the archetypal forms are protocols which we are actualizing and, in the process, transforming our illnesses and limitations.

At the end of a session I will often see a "past life" metaphor. Usually this is prompted by a pattern in the outer aura. When a Share the images, the client often recognizes the story or has a sense resonance that prompts an inner sense of resolution. Sometimes self forgiveness is needed. At other times there is an experience of epiphany, or resolution, which comes simply from hearing the story.

Concept

In the movies, the eminent appearance of an archetypal presence is communicated by a pervasive sound or silence in which the audience and the characters become aware that something big and unknown is about to happen. This event is usually reveals the plot, something essential about a character, a turning point, or the epiphany of the story.

Visually, it is the monster making its first appearance from the deep, or the appearance of a supernatural force. Meaningful coincidence, synchronicity, signals the appearance of an archetype. When we sense the archetypal energy field, it is pervasive and on the boundary of our normal and psychic awareness. Our only contact is our awareness. It is beyond time and completely present.

When we live our "life story" as our identify, our perception confirms that as reality. When we shift into our soul self, we see our movie as an archetypal drama and our fantasy miasmas convert to clarity.

Process

The appearance of the archetypal energy field in the context of Noetic Balancing usually comes with a specific purpose. Generally, your response is simply to participate in the apparent agenda. Engage the energy field, hold your focus, and surrender while maintaining your center.

Use metaphor and symbol to translate your experience on this level. The information you receive is rarely sequential. The archetype makes itself evident in order to adjust destiny, often in the form of a paradigm shift. Examples range from a simple adjustment, much like setting one's watch or straightening a picture. Other times, information appears which you convey to the client by describing what you see. Avoid interpretation. The client may respond to the information in an attempt to question or clarify. The client's request often elicits more information, insight, or clarification. Changes on the archetypal level may be as soft as a whisper or as dramatic as an earthquake or thunderstorm. In my experience, I often see a past-life metaphor, which I relate to the client as a story. Usually, as the client hears the story, balance occurs. Sometimes, the client experiences epiphany. The causal force is clearly synchronistic.

METAPHORIC LITERACY

Symbols and archetypes are codes that enable us to align and adjust the geometric matrix of consciousness. James Hillman and Edgar Cayce provide insight into what I call metaphoric literacy. By this, I mean a literacy that is living symbolism. We are not just deciphering, we are translating codes of multidimensional understanding while we are also adjusting the same codes. Our discernment changes the consciousness by the act of involvement. Whereas with Hillman and Cayce we explore how we adjust the matrix through meaning, with *the etheric* balancing and *light body* activation we change meaning by adjusting the matrix. As we adjust the matrix, our perception changes our reality.

James Hillman

Hillman developed what he calls the "acorn" theory of human development. In short, he says that the archetype of the adult lives in the child and that childhood tendencies are often the result of a child's consciousness seeing within itself an adult destiny. Concern or consternation in the child may have nothing to do with current events. Instead, they are an inner vision of future events. He gave the example of Monolete, the famous bull fighter, hiding in the folds of his mother's skirts, seemingly a shy, frightened child. In the context of his adult vocation, we see that he had reason for his fear and was practicing with his cape as a means to guide the bull of the future. Often we see in children's play the rehearsal of future destiny. If you were counseling Monolete you might tell him a story of a bullfighter vanquishing the most terrifying bulls.

Our inner wisdom carries out the commission of our soul to actualize our destiny. Another helpful Hillman concept is found in the phrase "the soul pathologizes." The metaphor of pathology reflects the destiny and reveals the deeper mission that the individual is attempting to fulfill. In this sense, the pathology symbolically reveals the intention of the client. From this perspective, the pathology is the healing. By facilitating the client's intention, the pathology is transformed and the soul gains greater substance. Hillman calls this process "soul making." While the physician pursues the pathology medically, the complementary healer facilitates the soul-awakening that is embedded in the metaphor of the disease.

As a process of noetic balancing, ask the client to elaborate on the pathology, whether physical, mental, or emotional. In this exchange, you assist the client to amplify and illuminate the archetype that is being revealed through the pathology. As the client becomes aware of the symbolic truth embedded in the pathology, transformation often occurs. When it does not, there is a deeper level of judgment that needs forgiveness, or it is not yet time. The pathology reflects the shadow side of a thwarted soul urge. During the session, the client becomes aware of the thwarted soul urge. Healing and forgiveness occur when the metaphor of the pathology becomes conscious. The metaphor resolves the tension between the pathology and the indexed soul purpose.

Edgar Cayce

To further help develop your metaphoric literacy, the Edgar Cayce readings present a concept of two archetypal patterns. One was called a "life seal," which symbolically depicts the destiny of the individual. It is an archetype of the life path. It is what Hillman might call the "acorn," and the existentialist might call the "a priori intention." The second archetypal form was called the "aura chart," which represents the character structure of the individual. In terms of the Cayce readings, the symbols of these charts reflect the strengths developed in past lives and then carried over to form the strengths and talents of this life.

In noetic balancing, each session forms a symbolic structure much like that described by Cayce. Themes and motifs emerge from the mosaic of trauma and transformation. At some point in the balancing, it becomes evident that the individual's life follows a karmic trail made up of areas the client desires to strengthen or fulfill.

Cayce's aura chart is a symbolic schematic of the individual's auric structure. Evaluation of the symbols contained in the aura chart, in terms of my balancing experience, reveals the genius of the human energy makeup. The fields of energy appear to carry an intelligence that is able to arrange itself in terms of power or in terms of the patterns that mute or block that power. As the client's awareness develops, and as sequential forgiveness builds energy, these patterns loosen. The structures of the psyche migrate into a more powerful relationship with each other. The noetic balancing brings forward past adaptations that are now limiting and transforms those patterns into contemporary power. Stumbling blocks become stepping stones.

The Cayce model of symbolic consciousness also provides a way of looking at experience and human development. Each event begins with a certain state of consciousness. The event challenges that state. The individual responds and emerges from that event with a new state of consciousness. For example, we may have lived a life in isolation, symbolized by a lone person. We yearn to be with others. We marry into an extended family. Through our experience with that family, we emerge with a sense of belonging and loving, symbolized by a radiant heart holding hands with a group of people. Again, by training our symbolic literacy, we develop an energy-based language gaining greater skill for translating patterns of energy into meaningful images.

APPLICATION

Balancing the noetic field in its simplest form is an application of living. Spirit, as it actualizes through form, is the unfolding of spirit into life. When we make a choice or take action, Spirit meets us. Simply going for a walk begins to balance us. Often by calling on our Holiness, or some form of alignment with our higher selves, and honoring our limiting choice or disturbing situation, we move to a greater balance. Higher consciousness must be asked. It will not inflict. As we resolve our experience, we empower our vertical center. The following are some ways to balance ourselves and to assist others, within the scope of what we have learned so far. The technique just described as Noetic Balancing requires more extensive training. These techniques are very powerful and need to be approached with care and respect.

Etheric Healing

Sometimes I experience a phenomenon that I call *etheric healing.* I experience an energy extension of my hands working directly on the etheric double of the body organs. Experiences similar to this are explained in Brennan's book, *Hands of Light,* and Powers' book, *Auric Mirror.* I can only explain this type of healing as an altered state of consciousness in which my awareness expands from my physical body to include my etheric body. In that state, energy hands work on energy organs. When I work in this way, it is not something I will. A higher power, which comes to me through the energy of the Christ, promotes the action and does the work. How this occurs is a mystery to me. Of course, so is the classical aura balancing, or something like breathing.

Activating the Light Body

One way to promote activation of the client's light body during a Noetic Field Balancing:

- Complete the entire balancing and just before you close the field, place your pendulum in the client's crown center, chakra ten, with the intent

to activate the right spin for the highest good. The pendulum will rotate clockwise until it is finished.
- Then place the pendulum below the feet in chakra twelve, with the intent to activate the merkaba magnetic spin for the highest good. The pendulum will spin counter clockwise until it is finished. You may feel the acceleration through the central axis and the movement of the two vortexes.

Looking at Hands

1. Through a prayer, ask to be surrounded by the Light for the highest good.
2. Look at the palms of your hands and relax, allowing the reflective relationship to generate energy.
3. Reflect on the situation, circumstance or issue that is causing you concern. Forgive yourself for judging yourself. If you are aware of a specific judgment like, "I am no good because I failed," forgive yourself for that belief.
4. Take a deep breath and let go. Proceed to the next circumstance or awareness of judgment.

Hand Pendulum

The *hand pendulum* technique is a more complex variation of *looking at hands*. The pendulum is an effective focus for noetic balancing, and is safe when used in the technique described. For this technique only, hold the pendulum in one hand over the palm of the other hand.

1. Through a prayer, ask to be surrounded by the Light for the highest good.
2. First practice using the pendulum. Hold the pendulum in one hand suspended over the palm of the other hand. Practice allowing the pendulum to spin clockwise. This is a convention of balancing energy in your field. It may spin counter-clockwise. Visualize it spinning clockwise. At this point we are practicing a convention that means the same thing to your basic self and high self. A clockwise spin means balancing is occurring and when it stops the balancing of that focus is complete.
3. After calling in the Light and practicing, you are ready to begin. Hold the pendulum over your palm, call your Holiness forward and ask for connection with your high self.
4. See your body in a sphere of Light. Next, scan your body with the focus of your attention. As your attention finds an area that needs balancing,

the pendulum will spin clockwise. As it does, let go and relax; allow the light to do the work. If judgments appear, forgive yourself. When the rotation stops, scan for another point by directing your focus to other areas of your body or in the field around your body. You can start with areas of tension or discomfort, and then scan less apparent locations.
5. After you have moved through the physical body, scan around your body. The pendulum will spin clockwise, reflecting that there is an area that needs balancing, and that balancing has begun. Again, as images or feelings arise, be aware of your judgments, limiting beliefs, or the incident in which the choice or judgment was made, and forgive yourself. When the pendulum stops, move on.
6. Proceed in this way until there is no more movement. This will indicate you have done as much as you can with this technique. A balancing by a qualified practitioner will go further. Bless yourself. Place yourself, situations and relationships, hopes and dreams in the Light, take a deep breath and release. There is always a higher consciousness that is guiding your process.

Partner Focusing

For this method, sit opposite a partner. You will be taking turns in the facilitator and client role, using the Structural Symbolic Focusing Protocol.

1. Call in the Light to surround both of you for the highest good.
2. The practitioner will be a witness and make the focus statements from the protocol. For example, ask: "Share a time when you experienced being alone, afraid, powerless or hurt." The statement is sufficient; the practitioner must avoid any attempt to coach, counsel, or process. If your partner appears stuck, only repeat the statement. The client says whatever comes to mind while the facilitator listens with a reductive focus and says nothing. Maintaining eye contact is very helpful. After each step, both take a deep breath, and remain silent for a suitable length of time. Maintain eye contact, and ask if another time comes to mind. If not, proceed to the next statement. The client forgives self for any judgments or limiting beliefs.
3. When all of the statements are complete, change roles and repeat the process.
4. When both are done, take a moment to place everything and each other into the Light, maintain a moment of silent eye contact, and then thank each other.

Hand Scan Balancing

In this method, we will directly engage the energy field of another person with our hands. When aligned with higher consciousness, touching a block will promote balance. Again, we will use practitioner and client roles. The practitioner must proceed without any agenda for the client, or his or her own importance. This technique can be used as a stand-alone, or after a counseling session or conversation in which an associate shared some concern or difficulty. It is not a "fix-someone" or "be-important" technique. Be respectful, loving and cautious.

1. The client sits in a chair and the practitioner stands. Placing hands on the client's shoulders or over his/her head, palms toward the client, and call in the Light for the highest good.
2. Place one hand over the top of the client's head. Do not touch the body. Use the other hand to scan the energy field. As you feel or sense something hold your hand at that spot. You may feel movement. Hold your hand on that spot until it seems as if the balancing has occurred. You can switch hands for convenience of reach, or place your hands on opposite sides of the client's body. Cross over the shoulders or head for a few moments, asking again that the Light serve the client for the highest good. When you sense completion, you are done. One way you may sense completion is that you are unable to find any more locations upon which you can work. Another way is that the energy field will become smooth. You may feel a sense of well being and expanded energy. The person in the client role may feel blissful, centered and relaxed.
3. Change roles and complete the same process.

PROTOCOLS

As we have discussed, we bind our energy through sequential processes. For that reason, the protocol of therapy may be more important than the content. The content certainly carries the frequency, or identification through which we locate and engage blocks. However, it is through our psychological traveling, and re-sequencing through awareness and choice, that we unfold the possibility of transformation. The following protocols have proven effective and useful in my practice.

Alignment

The protocol for aligning to the noetic field and activating your attunement is simple. It requires that you focus your attention, visualizing each element as it is added, to the best of your ability, and relaxing and releasing everything else. The noetic field matches you according to your understanding, imagery, and intention. When you have difficulty sensing, seeing, or experiencing your relationship to the nexus and noetic field, then your faith, intention, and surrender will work. Remember, in your nexus with the noetic field, you are more intelligent and compassionate than you are as an ego self alone.

If the following protocol seems to be too much, then instead: 1) be silent with your client for a moment, 2) honor his or her humanity, and 3) align yourself with unconditional positive regard. The numbers in this protocol correspond to the same numbers in the illustration.

1. In an attitude of reverence and surrender, begin with a prayer. Ask the higher power to be present and to surround you and the client, and surrender to that higher power. [The sequence is universal. Into this simple protocol, you insert the holy words that activate your attunement. A silent prayer is fine.]
2. Place your attention at the center of your brow, through your brow into the center of your head, and imagine a point of light. [You may see or experience a quality of energy, color, symbol or sound.]

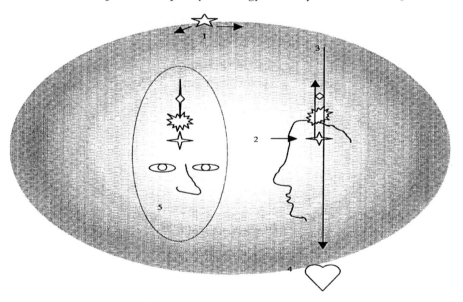

3. Direct your attention from the center of your head through the top of your head. [At some point, the noetic field will engage this focus, signified by a symbol, felt sense, or experience that is consistent with your spiritual orientation or archetypal nature. I often see the

Sanskrit word "Hu" or a dove with outstretched wings and head pointing toward the top of my head. To me, both signify the Holy Spirit.]
4. Bring your attention down through the top and center of your head into your heart. [Regard your heart as a chalice filling with energy from the noetic field and overflowing into your relationship with the client. You may see something other than a chalice, but generally it will be a receptacle, or receiving in nature.]
5. Direct your attention to your client while maintaining an awareness of your alignment. [Your aligned attention to the client through the noetic field activates a *soul circle*, which is a circular energy that links the souls of the client and the practitioner and contains the therapeutic process. It is a deep level of rapport.]

Reductive Focus

The *reductive focus protocol* unlocks sedimented beliefs or blocks. The sequence creates the necessary conditions for transformation and facilitates alignment with the soul.

As you practice the protocol and develop the skill of reduction, your mind develops into a perceptual organ of the soul. (Husserl did not use this exact description for his experience. He did, however, know he was changed by the practice of his *philosophy of science.)*

1. Begin with the alignment protocol.
2. Focus on the selected phenomenon (noema), excluding all else.
3. Deconstruct the sedimentation of beliefs, loosening your perceptual fixity.
4. Experientially discern the meaning (noesis).

Universal

The *universal protocol* provides a framework for applying techniques and procedures from compatible models that incorporate some form of reduction.

1. Begin with the alignment protocol.
2. Focus on cure as a soul-centering intentionality that is indexed to the issue or symptom.
3. Apply the technique, procedure, or protocol.

Foundation

The *foundation protocol* assists the client to move from a self-image, belief, or ego-center defined by external circumstances to a soul-centered knowing based on the experience of one's inherent goodness. The issue does not disappear. It remains worthy of consideration but no longer defines or dominates one's center.

1. Begin with the universal protocol.
2. Ask what the client is experiencing (felt sense).
3. Ask the client to take a breath, clear the air (energy field), and sharpen the focus on the reported experience.
4. Make a focusing statement. [For example, "Tell me a time when you tried to share your loving and couldn't." You may also perceive an image or have a sense, hunch, or insight from which you can form a focus statement. The client's insights may also serve to make focusing comments. The client may report information concerning an issue or a concern.]
5. Bring attention to or touch the point in the energy field around the client that expresses the distortion or block, or have the client touch the physical location. If nothing is apparent, just be present.
6. Assist the client to access and describe the traumatic moment: who did what to whom? Or, on the basis of that experience, how did the client diminish, judge, demean, or shame him/herself (noema)? Assist the client in self-forgiveness or reframe the judgment. [Audibly stating the forgiveness is important. A statement affirming one's self and the particular denied or suppressed virtue in relationship to the event is often a powerful support to the forgiveness process (reduction).]
7. Ask the client to take a deep breath to facilitate the release and the receptiveness to a response from higher consciousness.
8. Ask the client to give permission for higher consciousness or the Holy Spirit to touch into that injury or place of need and to give permission for that place to respond to that spiritual help.
9. Hold the space, and encourage the client to let go and follow the flow of the epiphany (noesis).

Insightful Focus

Notwithstanding that the road to mastery can be long and challenging, accessing the noetic field can be simple. In fact, it needs to be simple so that you can readily explore Noetic Balancing. The *insightful focus protocol* is a simple way to access information from the noetic field. It was developed from transcendental phenomenology, follows the same steps as the reductive focus protocol, and is used to align or bring insight to you and the client.

1. Focus on the image or statement that you want an answer for or understanding of (noema).
2. Inhale steadily and deeply while holding the noetic focus.
3. When the in-breath is maximum, hold it and focus intently on the noema.
4. Rapidly release the breath, and relax as totally as possible, letting go of the focus and releasing yourself into the noetic field (reduction).
5. Relax further while you allow understanding or insight to emerge (noesis).
6. Articulate (speak or journal) whatever occurs to you.

Re-Placing

In his book, *Look to the Mountain*, Greg Cajete, a foremost Native American scholar from the Santa Clara Pueblo in New Mexico, discusses the importance of place in indigenous learning. We speak of making a place for ourselves or finding our place. In the Native American experience, place is fundamental to a healthy spiritual and psychological orientation.

In the therapeutic relationship, I observed that clients were often required to give up who they were to get shelter, safety, nurture, esteem, or survival. They literally and symbolically had to give part of themselves to someone else who controlled what they needed. They had to relinquish their sense of place to be acculturated. Instead of the client having a sense of themselves in their own center or soul-space, the controlling person was in that space dictating how and what they should be. They had to "sell out" to bond themselves, so to speak. It was apparent to me that my clients had given away their space to the point of having lost their sense of owning their life or being their own person. They had no grounding. Symptomatically, they expressed this as a feeling of not belonging here, as if they were dropped from a space ship, illegitimate, or orphaned.

When one's sense of place is not sufficient, higher levels of integration appear to be limited. There is no place, in one's center or space, to anchor higher consciousness. Therapeutic changes do not seem to hold or work at all when the client's sense of place is insufficient. Without the compass provided by place, actualization is difficult and transformation is curtailed. The *re-placing protocol* strengthens the client's sense of place by retrieving, realigning, and reintegrating the "given-away self" with a place or center in present time. This technique is extremely helpful in situations of sexual abuse. Often the sense of one's self as victim, or one's self as permanently damaged, cannot be resolved until after the effective use of the *replacing* technique.

1. Find the initiating events when you gave a part of yourself away in exchange for safety, survival, power, nurture, esteem, or shelter.
2. Forgive yourself for abandoning or betraying yourself, and affirm yourself as your center.
3. Locate the symbolic self, that you actually gave away, in the field or image of the predatory person, that you "gave" the specific aspect of yourself away to. [Your self-image will appear embedded in the energy field or body of the other person.]
4. Begin a slow breath, and visualize the self you gave away that is embedded in the field of the predator. [It may appear as an image of you, color, shadow, or symbol. Your best criteria is that it seems like you and not the predator.]
5. As you continue the slow in-breath, see the given-away self traveling from the control person to you and entering through the top of your head into your physical body. It will go to its rightful place.
6. As you complete the breath, visualize the given-away self and the physical self-of-now in the same simultaneous place.
7. Hold your breath and continue visualizing both physical forms as one.
8. Rapidly exhale, let go, and totally relax. [The retrieved element merges with you in the present.]
9. Assess the field of the predator for other remnants of yourself. When all are retrieved, the predator will appear to recede, diminish or dissolve in some way. This indicates they no longer have a hold on you.

Making Even

I became aware of another perplexing issue similar to place. My usual approach either did not work or had minor effect. There was no evident shift in the client's felt sense or experience of self. I suspected that the blocks I had been addressing were an effect of a deeper concern or that a priority agenda held those forms in place.

I discovered that many times the priority agenda was some form of revenge. As long as the client wanted revenge, nothing would release, transform, or cure. Higher consciousness was unable or not permitted to assist. The target of the revenge can be someone else or one's self. It may look like "living up to someone else's expectations," or "proving oneself." Revenge holds a client in dualistic consciousness and, as such, prevents noetic-field access and soul-space alignment. Higher consciousness, being noninflictive and nonadversarial, has to stand by and cannot act as long as the client wants revenge.

We have a natural instinct to make ourselves whole. As a reversal of the natural instinct, revenge is an adversarial approach, which perpetuates wounding. When we center in our wound, wholeness becomes out of our reach. In contrast to "getting even," the *making even protocol* helps make whole.

1. Trace the early trauma.
2. Experience and own your victimization.
3. Accept the anger and rage resulting from the violation.
4. Determine whether the vengeful acts were directed at self or another.
5. Decide if you want to surrender your desire for revenge. If you give up your desire for revenge, you are not condoning the perpetrating behavior but changing your relationship to it. [As long as you want revenge the perpetrator controls your state of being. By wanting revenge, you perpetrate their action on yourself over and over. They only did it to you once.]
6. Forgive yourself for making revenge more important than the liberation of your own soul.
7. Allow the energy flow to complete itself while giving permission to your hurt place to receive spiritual intervention and give permission to the higher consciousness (Holy Spirit, Great Spirit, noetic field, universal compassion) to assist you deeply in your transformation. Have compassion for the victimizer.
8. Articulate any change in your subjective experience.
9. Check and see if there are remaining or additional elements of yourself embedded in the perpetrator's field. If so, repeat the process. If necessary, use the *replacing* protocol.

If appropriate, return to the original technique or procedures that appeared ineffective and that initially suggested revenge was the priority agenda and try it again. You can also combine this process with the *replacing* protocol.

Time Angel

The past continually cycles into the present. As we engage present challenges, we are also healing our past. We can translate current events into metaphor and look for causation in the past. When the past trauma awakens in our emotions and in our somatic memory, awareness brings transformation. As we deepen our awareness of self as energy, we become aware of a greater power for change within our noetic field.

Our vision of our past is very much alive within us. We can move noetically to any time or place when we once needed help. We still need the help. The goal is not to change the event. It is to change the quality of the event and our relationship to it. In a sense, as we interpret events and form our beliefs about ourselves in those events, we create holographic beings that are replicas of ourselves at those times. This phenomenon is similar to Callahan's "holons." When these *orphans* are created with insufficient loving, a vital aspect of our life force is caught in the dimension of the past. Once created, the location of these "holographic orphans" is in the unconscious field around our physical body.

In this protocol, the client is guided through a journey to her past. The goal of the journey is to find her *orphans* who needed someone like herself to be present, supportive, engaged, and loving. You can also use this protocol on yourself. To make it easier to read, the *time angel protocol* is presented as if to a female client. If appropriate, re-cast as a male client.

1. Relax and close your eyes while we ask for the presence of the Holy Spirit or the Light for the highest good. [Essentially, this is a prayer for guidance, protection, healing, and engaging the noetic field at a level that knows the highest good of the client and the practitioner.]
2. Imagine that you are traveling into your past. In this journey, you are looking for past selves who needed you as you are now. The goal is to be your self-of-now with your self-of-then. At some point, you will sense or see the self-of-then that needs you. Take your time. Observe.
3. As your self-of-then becomes clearer, describe that persona as distinct from the self-of-now, i.e., what is she wearing, what is on her feet, etc? How is her hair fixed? How old ..., what fragrances ..., time of day ..., inside ..., outside ..., time of year ... ? Engage all of your senses.
4. When your self-of-then becomes clear and more delineated and seems to take on a substance, a reality, see your self-of-now and your self-of-then together in that place and time. Be cautious. Give your self-of-then time to respond. She may be timid or somewhat frightened. If she does not recognize you, introduce yourself. Explain that you are her self-of-the-future and that you are there to help.
5. Slowly wait for her to approach you or begin to relax with your presence. See if you can reach out and touch her. If touch is allowed, explore holding her in your arms and fill her with your loving. This may take awhile.

6. When you sense that the loving is working, invite your self-of-then, if it seems appropriate, to forgive herself for any way that she believes she is unlovable, powerless, or inadequate because of the current circumstances or anything that may have happened. Have her forgive herself for any self-shame or blame. After the forgiveness, have her let it all go, and fill those spaces with more loving.
7. When the time seems right, tell your self-of-then that you must return to your time. Tell her that she can call you whenever she needs you. Or, she can return to the present with you, knowing that the two of you will merge.
8. Return to the present, take a deep breath, and see yourself as a light body containing your physical body. Be aware of what you are experiencing, and slowly open your eyes.

The name of this protocol honors an experience that I had with a client. When she was a small child, she was locked away in a room. The room was warm enough. She had a bed. Food was left for her, and she had a pot that she could use as a toilet. As I was guiding her in this process, we were just at the point when I said, "Now have the self-of-now enter the room with the self-of-then." She suddenly exclaimed, "Oh! I'm the one!" She said she survived those times because an angel had come to her. The angel held her and filled her with loving. When I had her enter the room, she said that she realized that the angel who had come to her was herself.

All the faculties are present in adult life to travel the time line as it is imaged into the holographic meaning-structures within the individual. Awakening to the transcendental dimension is like being "born again" into our wholeness. Time travel allows us to heal and transform our past, which creates a present that is as if we had lived the healed past. In a manner of speaking, we become our own parents. We move as the soul-of-itself and enter into whatever the time-bound self needs. As we awaken into the depth and wholeness of who we are, the events and beliefs appear in perspective. We see our life as a continual enhancement of the soul.

Structural Symbolic Focusing

Each consciousness center, or chakra, differentiates in its psychospiritual function into specialized areas. Each center serves the soul's activity in specialized ways. As a result, each center will characteristically contain blocking beliefs related to those functions. For example, when we try to share our loving and cannot, the beliefs we form in response to that trauma become blocks in the energy field near the heart center.

Begin with the alignment protocol. Each of the following focus statements provides a point of engagement. The focus statement draws a response from the client. This is an associative or resonant response, so whatever occurs to the client provides the next step. The focus statement and resonant response engages the intelligence and compassion of the noetic field. The focus statements are arranged in a particular sequence to optimize the therapeutic development of the energy field. For that reason, I recommend that you guide your progression according to the sequence given.

Insert each of the following focus statements into step four of the Foundation protocol. As content emerges, make any minor modifications that enable the process. Complete the entire Foundation Protocol for each block that emerges.

Solar plexus. Tell me about a time when you were alone, afraid, abandoned, hurt, or experienced guilt or shame.

Feet and knees. Tell me about a time when you were confused or didn't understand, felt unsupported, had no sense of place, or didn't belong.

Spleen and root. Tell me about a time when you judged your sexuality or creativity, had resentment, or needed revenge.

Heart. Tell me about a time when you had regret, felt disappointed or betrayed, or tried to share your loving and couldn't.

Throat and mouth. Tell me about a time when you had difficulty speaking, or because you spoke.

Eyes and ears. Tell me about a time when you saw or heard something that was painful, disturbing, or frightening.

When you are sensitive to the energy field, you will be aware of, or sense, the realignment of the client into soul-space and the enhanced flow of energy. Asking clients what they are experiencing provides a reference point and anchors the transformation. Depending on the level of therapy, this protocol may not require specific attention to each center. Rapport in the noetic field while asking the focus statements may be sufficient.

Symbolic Resonance

Symbolic resonance is a term I borrowed from Roger Wolger and his approach to regression therapy (past life). Simply stated, symbols resonate like piano strings: a note struck in one octave will resonate with the same note in another octave. The resonant consciousness opens memory fields from the past. The past experience appears as a structure in the field, forming as an intentionality that we must fulfill or complete in a present experience. The symptom is a resonant call to the past for awareness, fulfillment, and transformation.

For example, I was listening to a client's story. We had approached her situation from several perspectives, and nothing seemed to help. I suspected something deeper. As I listened, I heard the phrase "No matter what I do, it will never be enough." I asked her to close her eyes and repeat the phrase, letting go of anything else that tried to catch her attention. She said she experienced an inner vision, which appeared to be a past-life metaphor. She saw herself as a small child. Her mother had died and her father did what he could but did not have much time for her. She felt alone, abandoned, and unwanted—insufficient for meeting life's challenges. I asked her to go to her time of death. She found herself hovering over her corpse which had a sword piercing her neck into her shoulder. She had also complained of neck and shoulder pain. Her dying thought was, "Whatever I do, I will never be enough."

She had an element of revenge as well. In this case, she directed it toward herself. I always treat "past lives" as accurate and an appropriate metaphor. By doing so, I can avoid deciding whether or not it was an actual past life or whether or not we have past lives, and get on with the therapeutic process. As my teacher used to say, "We have to spend our eternity somewhere."

In summary, the protocol is:

1. Listen for the resonant phrase.
2. Direct the client to focus on it, and with closed eyes, repeat it over and over until it elicits a felt shift or image. Have the client articulate the felt sense and image.
3. Elaborate until epiphany occurs.
4. Elaborate in terms of understanding and current circumstances.
5. Conduct self-forgiveness, if appropriate.

A PASSAGE INTO DAY

By engaging the healing energies of life through Noetic Balancing, we open new doors to our spiritual understanding and graceful living. This offers a point of departure for exploring a larger perspective of human reality and the implications that it holds for our well-being. We are wondrous even in our most challenged moments. Ralph Waldo Emerson believed that we have within us all the wisdom of nature and the universe. If that is so, our injuries foretell our healing and our limitations foretell our expansiveness. In this universe of energy, consider that therapy is a place where souls meet and impersonal intimacy reclaims its forgotten selves until all exists in a sea of loving.

Our evolving mastery unfolds a deeper relationship to self and spirit. In the teachings of Hermes and Pythagorus, we find kindred spirits, offering access to the mystery. We find keys to the formation of the universe and our humanity, as a microcosm, an "image and likeness." They offer an invitation to join a lineage that began with the first breath, unfolding into the present creation. This lineage culminates in Jesus the Christ, who fully awakened as the Christ within the physical form. This changed us. The potential of our Holiness activates our genetic possibility. Though it is not clearly apparent, we live in a new day and new dawn, and are witnessing a planetary re-birth. As we choose a new baseline, we become conscious agents of this transformation. The foot prints of eternity become many.

When we meet
in the heart of the creator,
our wounds
become a warrior's footprint,
our trials and tribulations
become a healing balm,
our dark night,
a passage into day.

Chapter Seven

ZERO POINT INDEXING

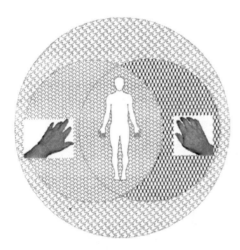

As *noetic practitioners*, experience is our greatest teacher. As we deepen in our capacity to center and observe, our physical and spiritual senses become increasingly refined. We trust our capacity to see and sense the underlying matrix from which physical life unfolds. Our response to challenges bypasses the function of defining who we believe we are and, instead, spontaneously accesses the wisdom of all. We are well into a path of transforming our sense of self from an externally programmed sociopolitical and environmental construct to a psychology of self based on a spiritual sense that intrinsically, seamlessly, and experientially merges with All That Is. We often experience this as a felt kinship with the Source of life and existence. Our genetic nature redistributes itself as a means of mediating the increasing sensory input of unconditioned, yet intentional reality. When we exercise our ability to touch patterns in the field matrix, through an intention to resolve the pattern, while dropping into a profound level of center, a transformation in reality occurs, enhancing our capacity to live as our greater self. Living from our greater self increasingly transforms our life from a *fear* or *excuse based reality* to a *grace based reality*.

Our genetic nature is also threefold. As a morphogenetic field, our genetic structure mediates between the environment in which we live and our spiritual nature. The threefold genetic nature is duality in unity. Our kinship with God is a genetic relationship. As a result, our transformational process stimulates greater change in the form and quality of our self as organism. We are just beginning to realize and appreciate the capacity of our physical body as an instrument of spiritual consciousness.

Our organism is such that its frequency changes depending on our attunement. Each shift in consciousness corresponds to a different brain frequency. *Beta* is frequencies of 14-28 cycles per second. Our brain is at these frequencies when we are talking. *Alpha* runs from 7-14 cps and is a bridge or transition. These are the frequencies of meditation or healing that is the "running of energy." *Theta* is 4-7 cps, the frequencies of deep relaxation, peace, causation, intention, God, connectedness. *Theta* is the frequency of *zero point*, or *witness*. *Delta* is 0-4 cps. This frequency is that of deep sleep and knowing. *Gamma* is 40-5000 cps and occurs when we are binding sensory input into unitary objects. Going in and up into God automatically shifts the brain into Theta. When the new reality manifests, Gamma waves are present. The morphogenetic field is binding new structure. Our physiology increasingly conforms to its innate capacity to bridge heaven and earth and thereby initiate resolution through the transformation of reality.

Our conscious and unconscious creations cycle back to us, mirrored from the life-field. So, all creation in general, and all of our creations in particular, are intentional structures that we can locate through the indexed relationship of form and spirit. Each form has a point and counterpoint. When the creation is imbalanced, or distorted, tension exists. Congruency reflects as balance. This is review, of course, but it helps to reconsider the basics as we move through various applications.

Application One

You have had many experiences of connectedness. Perhaps it was a moment as you stood on the beach and watched the sunset, or, when you stood on a mountain top. You saw the tree tops below and beyond into the distant valley. You may have stood silently in the aspen grove, transfixed by the gentle sound of the wind through the leaves and felt the life of the trees as one being. Perhaps you held a baby in your arms, sharing a transfixed moment looking into her smiling eyes. Remember the many heartfelt moments that resolved hurt, despair, loneliness. This is connectedness. This is kinship with All That Is. In connectedness you awaken your kinship as a genetic inheritance.

Shift your focus now into your heart. As your heart opens, expand that energy around your body. Using your fingertips, actually touch the heart frequency that now permeates the field around your body. Sense the movement in you and around your body—the sensations, feelings, emotions, images. Take a deep breath and relax, dropping farther within your body and deeper out into this field around your body. Choose another point of contact in the frequency of the heart field around your body and touch it with your fingertips. Choose two points and use both hands. Take a deep breath and let go. Drop into the depths of your connectedness.

Reflect on your heat field, amplifying the sensitivity of love that is present as your spiritually touch into your heart and physically touch the field activation of your heart. Your reflections amplify this energy. Now, focus into the light in the center of you head. If you do not see a light, imagine one. Direct your heart energy into the center of your head, expanding the light until it surrounds your head, surrounds your body. With your fingertips, touch this energy in the field around your body. Be aware of what you experience.

CONTEXTING

Contexting is a term I use to open a space in which a given reality can unfold. The context arises out of our *reality intent*. This is similar to bracketing, a term for phenomenological reduction. You focus on one thing with the exclusion of all else. The application is sweeping. A simple contexting occurs when we change the emotional atmosphere of any location or state of mind with attitude. Appreciations will re-context any situation or circumstance from adversity into wholeness. When I begin any class or session, I align with the highest consciousness, establishing a spiritual presence as the context. Our everyday context is reflected back to us from the mirror of life. When we want to change a reality, the context emerges that supports that change. We do this by directing our intent into the wholeness, or All That Is, into God. How we *context* is important. We can approach therapy as *problem based* or *reality based*. Both are served by centering into zero *point*. In zero point, we become nothing. While our ego may appear to be intact and present, in *zero point* we are not defined by any reflectivity. In zero point, our sense of self as a *greater* or *unified self* is maximized. *Zero point* maximizes our creative valence for changing reality, for transformation. Witnessing from *zero point* in itself is a powerful transformer.

In my experience with clients, either personally or at a distance (phone), I see the field matrix as a touch screen showing me the active elements. The active elements are those fixed patterns that reflect the beliefs or conditions that form the points of contact for shifting the reality. *Zero point* describes the experience of centering, or radical witness. We become so transparent that we are nothing (ego viewpoint). At *zero point*, the ego sense of "I" dissolves into "this I Am." It is the individual experience of the All That Is. In this state, universal wisdom and unconditional love are a unified presence in which my sense of self merges with all. I and the unified field are one.

When we are at *zero point*, we exist in the ultimate present, ultimate witness, the *power of now*. When we truly center, we open a dimensional vortex to all possibilities. We move our axis of power out of the ego time line and into creative space. It is from this space that our lives are manifest. It is from this center that we embrace life as union. In our center, life and spirit breathe through us and the reflected self drops away. In this place of nothing, we are all. We are each other. From our place of unity, we are observing our place of difference. Out of zero point our sense of kinship unfolds to invite us inward to Source and outward into intimacy with all that is. When we do, all must reconcile itself with its Source. Ultimately the created universe is indexed to the un-manifest Source. So, I continue to discuss this as if I can. We can discuss this through our unity. I remind you and you elaborate through your kinship with All That Is, with God.

Application Two

Create a sense of yourself in the ball of light in the center of your head. You can do this by imagining a ball of light in the center of your head and seeing an image of yourself in the ball of light. As you experience a sense of self within the ball of light, move through the top of your head, and as you do see a column of light that travels through the axis (spine) of your body into the earth and out through the top of your head. Follow the column of light out through the top of your head into the highest realm that you can imagine. If you like, see yourself in a field of pearlescent white light high above your physical self, and feel the undulating patterns of living love. You are connecting with the living love of All That Is, the living love of the God field. You can ask for an image or awareness of this reality to appear to you in a form that you can understand and you can speak to it: Say, "Send this energy of living love down into my heart, filling every cell of my body with living love. Surround my body and fill my space with living love." Observe and appreciate this action as it occurs. Affirm it so and give thanks. With your physical hands, touch the frequency of this energy in the field around your body with your fingertips. Take a deep breath, relax, and move with the presence that is in your field. See your mind as a stone dropping into a pool of water.

INDEXING

An index is a measure. In this case the issue and the intention that informed the action that created the issue is a measure of *issue* relative to *essence.* All actions and forms come from intention. The basic intention comes from our innate nature which is to fulfill or actualize our essence. We experience essence as kinship with All That Is or God. In the language of phenomenology this would express as noema (form) to noesis (essence). Deconstruction of the form reveals the essence. Energetically, the form collapses into the wholeness.

An imbalance in the field occurs when a congruent intentional force is subjected to a reversal. We choose to reverse our field specific to a given event when we believe the reflecting appearance is the true reality. We create a belief that the reflection is true. Our virtue reverses through our adverse choice. Adverse does not necessarily mean negative, as in bad. Good and bad in the field reflect to the same index spiritually. Good fulfills itself through negative and positive experience. Our belief in reflected self concept forms, or accretes, more frequencies on what we can call a *replicate self.* The *replicate self* is a reversal, or mirror image, of the soul self and plays a part in actualizing the soul's agenda. The *replicate self* can never fulfill, so we learn through contrast, the indexing of replicate to true self. We call these patterns *replicates* because they pose as genuine self, yet they oppose genuine fulfillment because they are fixed on the reflection, on the mirrored self image. Any time we mistake our reflection for truth, we pull our awareness and identity of self away from our truth. As we become sensitive to these differentiations of frequencies, we can expand our ability to shift these realities. Through our sensitivity, we can simultaneously attune to a global sense of center. Ego is a thing. Our true sense of self is referenced into the nothingness—large essence, small thing-ness. Basically, when we locate the point and counterpoint (through two hand touch), while at zero point, we can collapse the distortion by placing our intention into the wholeness, into God. Again, the goal is not to fix the problem. The problem is the result of a *reality set*; when we change that *set*, the *reality* changes. The motive to fix the problem, as an outer directed force, chooses a reality of *more of the same.* We may prefer the continuity. We like it as it is.

In Theta, we focus the intent into God. In Gamma, the elements are reorganized into a congruent pattern. Use imagination and will to create the connecting consciousness. We can look at this a *re-contexting.*

Application Three

Connect to your kinship with God, All That Is. Focus on a disturbance, imbalance, issue or consternation. Imagine it as an energetic pattern in the field around your body, and touch it with your fingers. Or, scan with one of your hands, then engage the frequency pattern with your touch. Your intention will select for the energy field of your disturbance. It will always "be at hand." With your other hand, find a contact that reveals itself as a counterpoint to your disturbance or one that amplifies the disturbance. One contact is in your replicate field and the other is in your congruent field. You are indexing the disturbance through touch in the matrix of your field. Allow the touch to amplify, while you observe and center into your connectedness, your kinship. See your intention to change the reality of your disturbance. As you see the stone of your mind drop into a pond, release the intention, and see yourself drop into the ocean of All That Is, drop into the God field of living love. Follow the movement of your experience. No expectations. You are living at zero point.

SELF MORPHOGENETIC

In terms of Noetic Balancing, I look at the matrix from the perspective of the soul and ego. The ego pattern is based on reversals of the soul pattern, or reflection, and, as such, is a reversal. This means that the soul intention is caught in reflection and bound in a thought, archetype or belief, as reversed programming. When we connect with a disturbance in the matrix, we find a complementary spot that increases the disturbance. This is a resource point. The sense of disturbance increases because the *light*, or *soul matrix*, begins to amplify the imbalance as an element of the balancing process. It wants to fulfill through completion. By dropping down, the standing wave of the reversal collapses. Each distortion is indexed to a congruent intentionality from the wholeness.

In terms of the following diagram, we connect with the soul-matrix with one hand and the replicate matrix with the other hand. This is a magnetic or horizontal action. We then center our consciousness in zero point, or nothing, we transcend the wave form of the target pattern. The intention is to collapse or transform the limiting belief, aberration or injury. When we drop into the unity, the bracketed reality collapses into unity. It is gone, and reality shifts. The new reality results in healing or transformation because of the change in reality. This is a co-creative process, a collaboration. We collude in the reversals and collaborate in the transformations. We do our ten percent and God does its ninety. In the Bible, Jesus said, "Don't let the right had know what the left hand is doing" and "what you ask of the Father (All Parent) in secret is given openly and abundantly (give your intention into the wholeness)." For the transformation to complete, we must observe the change. We observe through seeing or feeling. We also "see" by measuring change through our felt sense before and after, or suds (subjective units of distress). Our ten percent is to engage the two points selected by our transformational intention, center, and then drop into the wholeness (zero point)

The diagram depicts the soul-matrix and the replicate-matrix in the self morphogenetic. The soul matrix consists of morphogenetic information that has been resolved and integrated into a coherent frequency with Source. The replicate-matrix is the morphogenetic information of unresolved issues or works in progress. The replicate information is based on soul-self patterning, but is reversed in some way. In other words, the form is based on reflection. For example, I decide in this life I want to develop a deep and lasting love relationship with another individual. We have karma from relationships based on using the other person to make us worthy, get what we need or as a Source of our spirituality. We can also acquire this program from our family of origin. Consequently our self concept becomes a replicate of the true-self, using the information from the karmic or developmental reversals. Our intentional drive is to resolve and transform the replicate morphogenetic field and replace it with a congruent field. A quick way is to touch the frequency of the true self with one hand and the replicate with the other. You can sense subtle energies, so you can feel the measure of the two. If you can't, intention will do. You then engage the wholeness, and let go into that wholeness and observe from this zero point. You will experience a shift in reality. This can be done by the practitioner or the practitioner can guide the client.

As we form beliefs and concepts based on the dualistic reality of physical life, a "shadow" matrix develops. Essentially, this is the morphogenetic field of all our choices and beliefs. We develop as self-concept based on dualistic reflections. The more these reflections tell us that we are other than our soul self, the more alienated and outer directed we feel. We increasingly need to reinforce our sense of belonging and place with external forms and co-dependent relationships. All limiting and distorted beliefs are referenced or indexed to some aspect of self that is integral to the soul. For example, believing we are unworthy is indexed to "we are inherently worthy." We discover worthiness through the contrast of unworthiness. We experience this index as alienation, sadness, depression, etc. When we collapse the index, mature worthiness emerges—centered and congruent with essence-self.

From our center or soul-axis, we are motivated to actualize our nature and to return home. Our history is one of increasingly being drawn away from essence. Our sense of self becomes based on reversals or anti-soul frequencies. We mistake this reflected or replicate self as true-self. Perceived form is from the reflection. We create our reality through the interaction of essence and reflection. When physical self is based on the replicate self, there is a distortion between soul-axis matrix and physical matrix. When physical self is based on essence, congruence exists between soul-axis matrix and physical matrix.

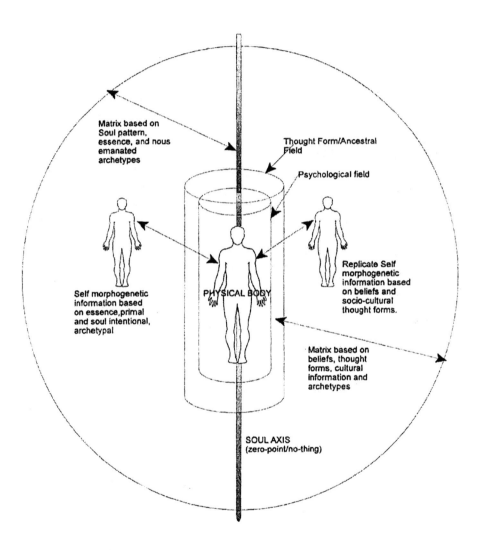

Application Four

Engage your connectedness, your sense of kinship with All That Is, with God. Amplify the experience of kinship with Source, with All. Touch this frequency in the field around your body. Center into the heart of God, while touching the matrix of God. Through your intention, with one hand touch the frequency of your replicate self. Your intention selects. As you explore the sensations and textures of touch, be aware of the experiential responses in your physical body, images and thoughts. As you proceed an experiential gestalt of your replicate self will form. You may see the gestalt visually or sense it as a presence in your space. If not, trust your intent for gestalt. You may actually sense your father, mother, aunts, uncles, brothers and sisters, ancestors, as you explore the morphogenetic contours of your replicate self. You may also feel a sense of tribe or nation.

As you continue to engage the replicate self morphogenetic with the touch of your hand, explore the self-morphogenetic of your true self, yourself as you unfold from essence into form. You will feel a sense of congruency with Soul. Explore the felt sense and sensations of living love, joy, peace, etc. Experience the sensorium of All That Is as a symphony of the soul, modulating through the cells, organs and fibers of your physical awareness. Experience the emotional movement and images that emerge from eternity into the individual awareness of self. Embrace the gestalt that emerges from this process.

When you are ready, refresh your sense of center, connectedness, kinship and let go. Choose the self you prefer and drop into the oceanic movement of All That Is. See the pebble of your mind drop into the pond of wholeness and watch the ripples expand into eternity. Move with the collapsing wave form. Ride your experience as your physical awareness accumulates the change in reality. Embrace yourself, your truth, your kinship. Let all else fall away. Give thanks.

CRYSTAL MATRIX

Another way to look at our *self morphogenetic* is as an undulating matrix of light that looks like liquid crystal. The matrix appears as three coherency fields (refer to earlier diagram). Of the interacting crystal fields, one comes out of the Source that we engage through our center and the others are magnetic, made up of the right and left hand of form. Everything in form is indexed to essence or first cause, the original template. Another way to say this is that a form is indexed to a source. Generally when I say this, I am referring to a spiritual Source; however, the source can be a reflected source, or magnetic source. The source of any apparent form can come from a reflective power or from the direct source, the Source of all. We could look at this as an archetypal or intentional force field. So we have form that is indexed to essence and form indexed to reflection, which is a replicate form, or false god. The reflected Source will collapse in the face of essence Source (love).

When we reference our self reflectively, the crystal matrix seems easily influenced by hypnotic information, prone to group think and propaganda. When we are centered in Soul, it filters, or reflects, external mental manipulating frequencies. Beliefs are thought forms, but not all thought forms are beliefs. Thought forms can exist independent of our beliefs. Thought forms may also believe they are real and can take on a form that resembles an entity. When we believe a thought form, we endow it with a reality. A zeitgeist is like thought forms accreted into an archetypal form. A zeitgeist is a *time spirit*, a *spirit of the times*.

By frequency entraining, a zeitgeist can influence an entire ethnic group, nation or the human race. The crystal body is extremely receptive to frequency influence. The influence is very subtle and easy to mistake as truth or one's own nature. The individual crystal matrix of one person can communicate with others through a sound/light sensing interaction. This data communication can form resonances that appear as mass hypnosis or group think. Masses of people can be controlled and mobilized in this way. Oppositional approaches such as fixing problems will have little effect and, in most cases, will amplify the influence of these fields. Negative forces can use these frequencies, causing "againstness", and thereby continuing to thrive on groups of people perceiving other groups as different and therefore against. They do not come from Source so they need the energy of opposition to fuel their existence.

The remedy is to align the crystal matrix with soul and to dissolve the mindset that seeks safety, love, power or health through fixing problems. Instead of fixing, we ask "What is the reality set that makes this problem possible, and what reality do I prefer?" Said another way, we are transforming the adversarial approach as a means of improving our quality of life. The crystal matrix rotates around an axis and on each facet and spectrum. When the axis is our center, the matrix has a high frequency. When the axis is fear or a replicate self, the resonance collaborates with lower frequencies as a paradigm of domination. When all is optimum, only soul frequencies and above pass or radiate, depending on karmic distortions, beliefs, trauma, programming, etc. Certain facets are susceptible to reversal and adverse relationships. When this crystal body is coherent and in soul resonance, life reflects a high degree of grace.

We can balance the crystal matrix, as we previously discussed, by engaging wholeness (centering), touching the distortion, and dropping our intention into the wholeness, and then observing. To do this, we can utilize touch through focused attention, our fingertips, or using a pendulum. The difference is that in each case our intention chooses the context of the balancing. This activity continues to surface distortion from the unconscious in the form of life challenges and discomfort. So we systematically continue to appreciate all indicators that reveal new areas from which to liberate ancient reservoirs of trapped energy. As we liberate these distortions and blocks, we incorporate the energy into our health, vitality and abundance and the distorted codes into wisdom. Similar to the archetypal level of balancing discussed earlier, this level of balancing is often silent. We center and focus our attention from and through *living love*. The measure of all transformation is the presence of love.

Application Five

Be with a friend, client, or colleague. Sit or stand. Engage your connectedness and through that kinship you are in rapport with each other. With your hand, touch the frequency of this rapport. You can sense it clearly with your touch, and in the rapport of the surrounding field. Give thanks for the presence of living love. Give thanks for the presence of the Christ and Holy Spirit, if you like. Give thanks for the presence of Allah, or the Buddha, if you like. Give thanks. Realize that this is your reality and that your colleague is a mirror within that realty as you are a mirror within hers, within his. There is nothing to fix, no problem to solve. Ask your colleague to tell you their concern. This is the intention you will give to God, All That is, through your connectedness, your kinship. You are involved in Divine collaboration to shift realty to one that is preferred. The intention brackets or selects the frequency and points of contact, the index, the reality transformation. With your fingertips touch the indexed points in the field of your colleague. You might touch the body, if that is where the field points are. You will feel the contact. As you find the contact points, align in your connectedness, in your center. Take a deep breath, and drop into the wholeness, the All That is. You are the stone dropping into the oceanic arms of All That Is. Move with the experience with your colleague. Ask what she/he is experiencing. What is your experience?

Chapter Eight

NATURE OF IMBALANCES

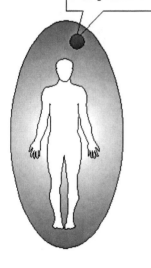

1. Intention to Action
2. Life Encounter
3. Reflection/Choice
4. Belief/Judgment
5. Field Construction
6. Thought form/Block

Blocks and imbalances help us answer the age-old questions: Who am I? What am I? What do I want? How do I fulfill my life? The more energized and integrated the noetic field, the faster the process. Transformation and realization can be instantaneous. The noetic field wants to be in balance. As we grow wiser, we are more attentive to the care and maintenance of ourselves as energy. Although these patterns in the field represent energy limitations, each one also holds a key to greater spiritual realization and strengthening. They are adversaries that become allies through our own transformational imperative. When aligned and balanced, the aura is a radiant energy, emanating living light. Because the noetic field serves the transformative agendas of the soul, it is constructed such that imbalances are functionally incorporated into our ego structure. At one level the ego takes the imbalance or distortion as a belief that is essential to one's identity. At another level, the construction is indexing a soul aim, an intentional agenda that the soul strives to fulfill. At yet another level the construction is a remedial or temporary solution which protects and provides limited stability while other aspects of the personality gain strength and experience. When the block is surrounded by sufficient experience, the noetic intelligence, through love, makes it available for transformation. The aura itself is capable of absorbing trauma, falsity, disease, and separation—all part of a process that results in adding purified experience to the soul. Psychological and spiritual wounds condense, even into physical disease, to assist us to complete the soul's imperative.

Access

The ways that imbalances function within the dynamics of the aura depend on the client's individual nature and the purpose, function, and content of the distorted energy. We engage the distortions through selective attention to the pattern or structure of energy. Each distortion is configured by a choice or belief, by a momentary choice in which we bind energy to a specific image. Once engaged, the story within these forms and patterns can be accessed symbolically. The symbols have important information concerning the purpose that was being pursued when the blockage occurred, the event itself, and the client's response.

Goal

Spirit supports us in our choices even when such choices cause us continued pain and separation. Because we are an expression of Spirit's process, it will not violate our choice. Yet it is vigilant to bring forward its living love, power, and wisdom to transform our energy as we allow it. In this sense, the darkness portends the light. Our trauma marks a location into which we will discover conscious divinity. This coming of the Light is an epiphany, the experience of transformation. It is a holy, sacramental event. Our injury is a sacrifice to the imperative to fulfill our divinity, our destiny.

Ultimately, each of us is an epiphany, a conscious, volitional coming of the Light. As soul, we give ourselves to incarnation, into this body, as a sacrifice to the realization and salvation of whom and what we are as an evolving, transforming divine expression.

CLINICAL GUIDANCE

Blocks and distortions in the aura are created by our response to circumstances. This response takes the form of belief. Empowering beliefs strengthen the field. Beliefs that are contrary to our innate love, joy, curiosity, enthusiasm, and intelligence contract or distort the flow of energy in the field. Distortions make the field susceptible to negative forms and influences. In short, our belief against self unfolds as a distortion in the energy field.

The following discussion is not a complete inventory of all blocks. It is a sampling of possible blocks to aid you to develop your thinking and understanding of the structure of distortions in the energy field and how to assist yourself and others in their release and balance. The discussion is to further your noetic development.

Appearance

The following diagram illustrates how imbalances might appear in the aura. This illustration gives a sense of the structural nature of distortions in the aura and a basis to further train our minds and develop ways of thinking and perceiving toward understanding our spiritual essence, psychological process, and physical experience as a reality of energy. For more illustrations, see Brennan's book, *Healing Hands*, and Leadbeater's book, *Man Visible and Invisible*.

A. Ceiling from Limiting Spiritual Belief

Affected Area. Etheric energy field and above the head.

Source. Religious belief can help and strengthen us in our faith and life. It can also limit. A dogmatic definition of what spirit is and how one experiences that spirit can structure a separation from any deeper or more transcendental spiritual reality. This belief can have experiential components and often does as the ceiling becomes more sophisticated. A ceiling can also be formed by a belief that we are rejected by or unacceptable to God.

Another Source of ceiling can come from being a devotee of a teacher who becomes the Source of the spiritual energy. The good news is that there may be a degree of genuine spiritual transmission. We may also, however, be held at that teacher's level of understanding or attainment.

I was working with a woman in the Noetic Balancing Practitioner class. She was Italian and Catholic. She was an excellent student with great potential; however, after leaving class, she felt like she lost her connection to Spirit. When we traced it back, we discovered that for her to belong to her Italian family, as a woman, she was forbidden to be a priest. With self forgiveness, it cleared immediately and now her alignment remains strong.

The basis of all these choices is the longing for a strong relationship with the Divine. In the Ten Commandments, we are admonished to have no other gods before us. Jesus said, Love God with all your mind, body, and spirit, and love your neighbor as yourself. The procedure to transform this aura distortion is to touch the longing for spiritual union or connection.

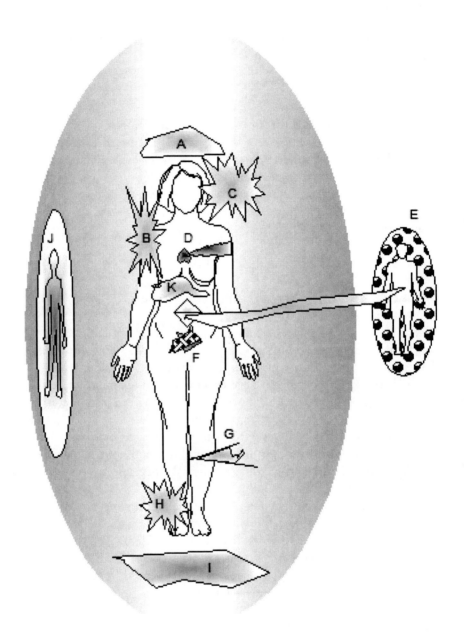

Guidance. Depending on the situation,

- I forgive myself for believing that I am personally rejected or unacceptable to God.
- I forgive myself for believing my teacher is the ultimate Source of my spirituality.
- I forgive myself for judging myself because my teacher turned out to be a fraud.
- I forgive myself for believing that I need to be attached to a teacher.
- I forgive myself for forgetting I am divine.
- I forgive myself for placing my judgments about the teacher's behavior in the way of my relationship to the Holy Spirit.

B. Fear or Extreme Worry

Affected Area. Emotional energy field and behind the head.

Source. Fear causes us to contract, which pulls us away from the universal field of energy and the comfort and support that it provides. We feel small. Often fear will contract the energy through the shoulder as if it might push us down or crush us at that point. Worry, which is a small fear, can over time contract the energy at the shoulders. The arm and shoulder energy is linked to the heart, so we might also see the symbolization as loss of heart or fear of reaching out.

Guidance

- Get in touch with your inherent urge to reach out to life and to engage life with your loving and enthusiasm.
- I forgive myself for believing I am powerless in my love and my ability to shoulder responsibility.
- I give myself permission and ask Divine Spirit to join with me in my love of life and shouldering my responsibilities.
- I forgive myself for believing that the only way to be safe when I experience fear is to contract.

C. Saw Something Horrible or Afraid to Face Something

Affected Area. Mental and emotional energy fields and in front of the face.

Source. Thought can create forms in the aura. In this case, she saw something at a young age that was extremely frightening. To protect herself she blocked the memory. In the long term, it may affect her eyes as it constricts, screens, and distorts the flow of energy. This block may also affect her in a way that makes her afraid to face her responsibilities or face a dangerous situation. *Not wanting to face* places the block, as a projection, in front of the face.

Guidance

- I forgive myself for judging my childhood choice to be safe, and for believing that it was the only way I had to protect myself.
- I forgive myself for blocking my vision and believing I am at fault or powerless.
- I forgive myself for shaping my center after the image of external danger.
- I forgive myself for denying my responsibility to choose on my own behalf.
- I give myself permission to see, and ask Divine Spirit to help me and stand with me in the face of difficult challenges.

D. Betrayal, Heartbreak

Affected Area. Emotional and mental energy fields and the heart.

Source. The lightning bolt symbolizes energy impacting the heart area. Betrayal or heartbreak might run both ways. The other person may carry and project anger corresponding to the damaged heart. This projection carries a force that amplifies any judgment we may already put on ourselves. It is an external psychic attack and an internal allowance or choice to be a target for that attack.

Betrayal and heartbreak can also come from an omission in life. Giving up or choosing not to continue one's growth and deepening of one's inner life can respond energetically and symbolically as a heart attack. We often mind other people's business as a means of protecting our sensitivity to caring or giving and receiving love. Ironically this behavior can over-stress and weaken our hearts.

Guidance

- I bring my focus into the awareness of my inherent loving, my need for intimacy, and my need to give and receive loving.

- In all cases, I honor the intention to have more love in my life.
- I forgive myself for believing that my love originates in someone else and that my love is not enough.
- I forgive myself for manipulating through my expectations, based on my beliefs of how others ought to act, in order for me to be okay or lovable.
- I forgive myself for not acting on behalf of my loving, playing it safe, and not taking a chance.
- I forgive myself for giving up and choosing to no longer grow or risk.
- I forgive myself for believing that the only way to be safe is to manage others.
- I forgive myself for believing that my judgment of the perpetrator, and my belief in revenge, will make me whole or better. (Sometimes it helps to forgive the perpetrator. In a sense you extend yourself forgiveness to the forgiveness of the perpetrator.)
- I give myself permission and give permission to the Light to enter my heart and make it strong.
- I give myself permission to realize and share from the worthiness, safety and power of my loving.

E. Attachment by Outside Control From Another

Affected Area. Cuts across all energy fields at the solar plexus.

Source. When we are in, or have been in, a relationship with someone who dominates or depends on us, an energy cord forms that acts like a conduit or a tether. Co-dependency is a symptom of these relationships. Often, we give up parts of ourselves to be loved or get something we need, like security, wealth, or safety. We actually place some of our energy with the individual representing what we need. This energy remains symbolically attached until we change the relationship, through self forgiveness, cutting the cord, or some similar ritual.

Guidance

- I forgive myself for defining myself by giving up parts of myself, believing that I was inadequate, and defining myself by my lack.

If you were the one who needed to be needed as the savior or needed to compensate through dominating another:

- I forgive myself for using someone else to feel good about myself.
- I forgive myself for believing that I lack sufficient strength and goodness in myself.
- I forgive myself for giving myself away and taking on the projection of another.
- Take a deep breath and breathe in your split-off part, or take a breath and release the other—whichever is appropriate. (See *Re-Placing* protocol in *Foot Prints of Eternity,* Chapter 7.)
- Visualize the cord between the two of you being severed.
- I give myself permission to receive the assistance of Divine Spirit to align my sense of self and security with my soul-self.
- See your space fill with light, and all attachments or need for attachments disperse.

F. Sexual Trauma

Affected Area. Sacral areas and organs related to sexuality and gender identity.

Source. The emotional and physical trauma of childhood violation, or from disrespectful or abusive intimacy. Occasionally there is a past-life component to this type of trauma. The judgment is often one of being to blame, especially in childhood, or a belief in one's unworthiness. Often the belief or judgment is gender related and accompanied by beliefs that one's body does not belong to one and that one is destined to live a role of victimization. A key judgment is often that one is permanently damaged.

Guidance.

We all have responsibility in terms of creating, promoting or allowing. That is about taking responsibility for the purpose of personal empowerment and changing your situation. The perpetrator also has choice and responsibility, and decided to violate you. The self-forgiveness is for what you judged or decided. When you judge, you continue the violation in your mind, independent of the perpetrator.

- I forgive myself for believing my body does not belong to me.
- I forgive myself for believing that I am permanently damaged.

- I forgive myself for believing that I am unclean or shameful because of what happened.
- I forgive myself for believing that what happened was my fault.
- I forgive myself for believing that I am destined, or doomed, to this type of intimacy.

These forgivenesses are, for the most part, the result of actual trauma. These types of blocks can also come from cultural attitudes that define gender roles and imply that your sexuality is a product, or commodity of the community.

- I forgive myself for believing it is a curse to be a woman.
- I forgive myself for believing the only way I can get what I need is through bartering my sexuality.

G. Old Leg Injury

Affected Area. Physical energy field and the place of the injury.

Source. Physical injury may not completely heal, or the subtle body may not properly realign or connect in the healing process. Sometimes emotional trauma and judgment about the cause of the injury or the way it happened may linger. The judgment might be as simple as not trusting ourselves physically or, in the case of the leg, believing we are not well supported in life.

Guidance.

- I enjoy being pain-free and I have reverence toward the miracle of my capacity to heal physically.
- I forgive myself for promoting this event through my arrogance or negativity toward another.

On the other hand, you may have been enjoying the freedom and joy of play and in your abandon, hurt yourself.

- I apologize to myself.

If someone else was involved, either consciously or unconsciously,

- I forgive everyone involved, for whatever reason.

Often, when we heal from a physical injury, the subtle body and the meridians spoken of in acupuncture remain severed. Forgiveness, visualizing light filling in the break, and receiving treatment from healing hands usually completes the healing in the subtle body.

- I reassure my leg and affirm my trust in its ability.

If there is a residual physical problem,

- Visualize red energy through the break while exerting mild tension on the area over a period of time.

Pain or numbness can be associated with a function for which there is judgment. To illustrate, my brother was home on leave before going to Viet Nam during the war. He commented that the index finger on his right hand went numb and that the numbness was moving up his right forearm. He was an excellent marksman and was being assigned as a sniper. I held his hand and forearm. I "saw" a target, so I ask him how he felt about the war. He believed that the war was wrong. This was difficult because he was a career soldier. He said that he felt conflicted. As soon as he said that, the feeling came back into his hand.

- I forgive myself for personally identifying with the war.

H. Wants to Kick Someone

Affected Area. Physical and emotional energy field and the foot.

Source. Blocks can have the symbology of a functional action. In this case, anger at someone manifests as wanting to kick someone. Actually kicking the person might change the energy, but probably would not clear it. In fact, it would create a further cause and effect regarding revenge. The block can remain as a grudge or regret. Perhaps the action engendered retaliation and continued separation. The vendetta can psychically bind the actor to the object of that action.

Anger and revenge come from a desire to make whole a circumstance in which we feel something was taken from us. Anger can stir us to action, but in the larger view, revenge does not heal or make whole.

Guidance

- I acknowledge my sense of injury and I forgive myself for wanting to damage another and seek revenge.
- I forgive myself for believing that damaging the perpetrator will make me whole.

Beneath the altercation is deep pain. The perpetrator is suffering. Until a healing bridge can be developed between the victim and the perpetrator, compassion is a good "step" forward.

- I place all concerned in the Light for the highest good.

I. Belief that One Has No Place or Space to Be Here

Affected Area. Etheric and mental energy fields and below the feet.

Source. A world that often neglects to love, criticizes, rarely complements, separates us from our mothers at birth, victimizes, or makes it tempting to sell ourselves out for what we need, promotes a belief that there is no place for us. Place is an important element in our spiritual compass. Family, community, and religion provide some sense of place. Place plays an important part in some indigenous cultures. We can also have a sense of spiritual place or legitimacy within ourselves. Religions that are heavy on shame may, however, make that experience difficult. We may feel like orphans or that we stepped off of a spaceship. We long to take our place and align with the reality of our spiritual home. Just as the ceiling can block the spiritual flow through the head, the lack of place can block the spiritual flow through the feet.

We all want to participate in and be part of others lives. Place is more than belonging, though that is part of it. Place meets a deep urge for spiritual legitimacy and having a divine point of reference. When we do not feel welcome and believe we do not have a place, it affects our spiritual compass.

Guidance

- I forgive myself for believing I am unworthy, unlovable, or that I am defective.
- I forgive myself for abandoning myself.

Your sense of not having a place will lead you to deeper spiritual initiation and to the ability to be in the world but not of it, which is an important step in our spiritual freedom and integrity.

- Take a breath and see yourself coming into your body and accepting your place in life and engaging the soul-space that is your eternal place.

J. Impinging Disincarnate Life Form

Affected Area. Attaches to the etheric and mental energy fields.

Source. Sometimes a disincarnate form may seek refuge or some other agenda through a vicarious relationship with us. The disincarnate individual may be confused or be strongly attached to a habit we are expressing. Our victimization and abnegation through substance use can make a place for such life forms.

Guidance

- Take some time to connect with your love and fulfillment through relationships with others worthy of your humanity.

This situation is similar to attachments, except the disincarnate individual is pulled into your aura. This could come from a time when you were weakened through illness or substance abuse. Usually, it is related to abnegation of your own authority through giving up or passing out. Generally, the disincarnate is confused, even lost, and needs guidance. It may also be connected through a vicarious addiction that you have in common.

- I forgive myself for times when I abdicated my consciousness or gave up.
- I forgive myself for using drugs or alcohol in a way that invited entity attachments into my field.
- I call on the Light to lift, counsel, and conduct the disincarnate on its way.

When the disincarnate individual resists, the prayer is more forceful and we ask for additional spiritual help. The request of Divine Spirit is one of clearing and strengthening you within your own beauty, power, authority, and integrity, and affirming your worthiness and ability to receive divine help.

K. Drug Residue

Affected Area. Physical, imaginal, and etheric energy fields, lung and heart area.

Source. Drugs in general leave a residue in the aura. This pattern is typical of recreational marijuana use. The residue has a sticky, hooking texture. Heavy tobacco smoking can also cause a residue that is less pronounced and often feels granular. Temperament and physical activity can affect the amount of drug use that becomes residue. The attitude and intention connected with one's use also has an effect. Drug use may be in one's karmic flow for a time.

Apart from any judgment about drug use, the residue takes up space, slows the energy flow, and keeps us from experiencing emotional pain so that we don't know we hurt, which blocks the flow of light into that area.

Drugs generally leave a residue that limits the health of your aura. Generally, we use drugs out of a spirit of adventure or curiosity, to numb ourselves from pain, or to avoid life. Prescription drugs can also leave residue. Sedatives used in surgery or pain killers for recovery or injury leave residue. When drug use is something in the past, the focus and spiritual energy can readily transmute the residue when permission to do so is truly given. Residue from prescription drug use is easier to balance.

Guidance. Depending on the context,

- I forgive myself for making myself numb, for numbing my pain, for avoiding life.
- I forgive myself for any unknown way that my drug use has been limiting or harmful.
- I forgive myself for making drugs more important than a genuine spiritual experience.

Some insight and wisdom may have been gained from drug use, especially in the context of spiritual ritual or intention. In that case,

- Acknowledge the good that was gained.

Neutrality is especially important in bringing light into any process of balancing drug residue.

- I thank myself for any wisdom or help I gained medically.
- I honor any assistance on my spiritual path that I gained.
- I affirm my inherent spirituality and the deeper wisdom that is not formed from the vehicle of external substances and that is an expression of my soul.
- My drug use does not make me or anyone else evil, and I forgive myself for any harm or limitation that I created, and I am moving on.
- I realize that my rationalizations for drug use are always deceptive, and I forgive myself, and surrender the entire matter to Divine Spirit and invite it to guide me.

INSIGHT

In the previous section, we explored blocks as imagined in the noetic field. In this section, I added a feature. When we align ourselves in witness and engage a block or distortion through touching with our hand, attention, or sight, and allow our awareness to open into our presence, we are available to "see" images, symbols, or narration that reflect the intentional vector that sustains, or that created, the block or distortion. With that in mind, we will explore the following diagram using the previous format, with the added feature of attaching an image to each area.

1. Ceiling created by harboring revenge

Affected Area. Above head and control chakra, preventing a nexus to higher center and Source.

Source. In this case the cleint is harboring revenge. He would like to kill the person who wronged him, get even.

Guidance. Revenge corrupts our natural drive to be made whole. Being made whole is a legal term in which the wronged party seeks some kind of redress from the party that damaged them or their property, or that took something from them. In this case the individual can be made whole by allowing karma to do the job. In that case they would not be cut off from Spirit. In these lower material worlds of duality, you cannot take revenge, because Holiness cannot inflict on Holiness. You shut the door to higher consciousness, and the repercussions are on you. Since the alleged perpetrator is also divine, attacking them is the same as attacking Spirit. This does not preclude being firm or forceful in you love and neutrality. When you give the perpetrator to God, karma will take care of it, sometimes rapidly. Revenge also places you in a relationship to the perpetrator such that you continue to be controlled by what occurred.

- I forgive myself for believing revenge is an effective way to be made whole.
- I forgive myself for believing that I have to harm _____ to avenge what happed to me.

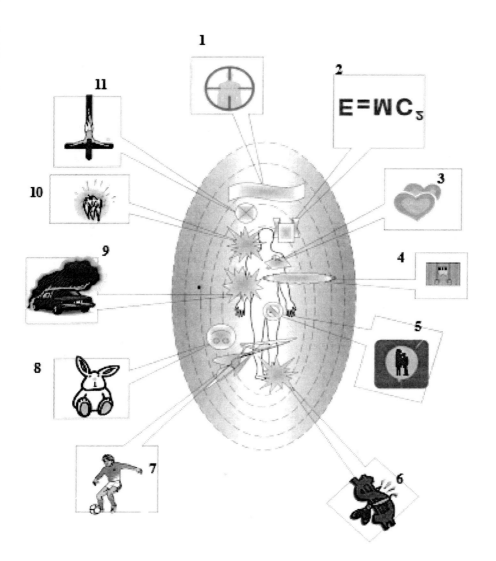

- I forgive myself for believing that _____ won't be held accountable if I don't get revenge.
- I forgive myself for believing that my well being is based on what happens to the other person.

The most effective action is to acknowledge the hurt, loss and damage this person did to you, or someone you love, and place them in the Light, give them to higher consciousness, adopt an observer relationship to them. Watch and see what happens when you give them up to the universal.

2. Humiliation In Science Class

Affected area. Mental capacity, especially in the formation of beliefs that one is not smart or is challenged in the sciences.

Source. In an environment of competitive learning and varying rates of development, performance in a given subject can be affected even if a person has potential in that area. In this case, let's say that this individual was in a science class and everyone was doing a chemistry experiment that on the surface seemed easy. The individual made an error in a measurement and spoiled the results. Everyone else did fine. Someone in the class ridiculed them in jest. The teacher unthinkingly joined in with a mild quip. Say this individual had not been getting enough sleep for a while and, though they wanted to do well, was not doing well. Consequently, this event hit him hard and he decided school was useless, and that he was not smart enough to understand technical material.

Guidance. Once the belief or judgment forms, it drops into the unconscious and out into the energy field, taking up residence in the perceptual matrix. In this case, actually distorting the energy matrix around the part of the brain that processes technical material influences the thinking processes.

- I forgive myself for believing that I am stupid and that it is no use to try, because of what happened.
- I forgive myself for judging myself because the experiment did not go well.

3. Divided Heart

Affected area. Psychic split in heart due to fear and attraction. Involved in relationship with several women at the same time. Confusion over being in love with more than one woman at a time. Pressure on physical heart due to emotional conflict and mental confusion.

Source. Fear of commitment while feeling a sense of safety in intimacy. Father was overwhelmed by the responsibilities of family and mother abandoned herself through her obligation to her husband. Both parents looked to son for vicarious fulfillment. Pressure to succeed, get married, have children. To him that meant his life would be over through commitment.

Guidance. The key is always resolving one's relationship to self, and becoming secure in personal worth and identity through relationship to God and soul. Intimacy becomes an addiction that numbs the pain and fear of being alone or abandoned.

- I forgive myself for believing my worth and safety are based on intimacy with others.
- I forgive myself for not loving and trusting myself.
- I forgive myself for believing I am not sufficient in and of myself.
- I forgive myself for believing that I must abandon myself in order to have a committed relationship.
- I forgive myself for judging myself and believing that I can only be safe through intimacy.
- I forgive myself for believing that I can only be intimate with myself through being intimate with someone else.

4. Arrested by Police.

Affected area. Heart, lungs and left arm.

Source. He stole a toy from the dime store when he was ten. The storekeeper caught him and called the police. His parents had to come to the station and get him. He was from an upper middle class family with high standards and low contact. He felt a deep need for something that he couldn't define at the time. He needed to fill an empty space. Actually, he felt unloved, unlovable, and that his parents didn't really care. He also had a high sense of adventure. When his parents took him home, he was severely reprimanded, reinforcing his own judgments. He felt hopeless.

Guidance. This is actually two events. Getting caught stealing and being scolded by his parents.

- I forgive myself for believing that my adventuresome spirit is bad and should be suppressed.
- I forgive myself for believing I am unlovable.
- I forgive myself for believing that getting the love I need is beyond hope.

5. Sexual Violation

Affected area. Genitals, anal, sacral area.

Source. As a young adolescent, he had an uncle who hired him to help in the yard. On breaks he would invite him into the tool shed and fondle him. This led to sexual penetration. The uncle would overpay him for the yard work and swear him to secrecy. Consequently, he had confusion about his sexuality and a great deal of shame and guilt.

Guidance. The tendency is to suppress one's anger with shame and begin to doubt one's own wholesomeness. Often, the victim believes he is permanently damaged and will act out aggressively and inappropriately in physical or sexual ways.

- I forgive myself for believing I am permanently damaged because of what happened.
- I forgive myself for believing I am shameful or unclean because of what happened.
- I forgive myself for believing my body does not belong to me.
- I forgive myself for believing that my body cannot know the experience of unconditional love.
- I forgive myself for believing that intimacy is always dangerous.

6. Cut off From Financial Support

Affected area. Feet area and flow of energy up through feet.

Source. Belief that there are limited resources and that one will always be unable to do more than just have enough. Grew up in a family that for generations had been in lower economic brackets and had cultural pride in their poverty.

Guidance.

- I forgive myself for believing that I will always just have enough money for what I need.

- I forgive myself for believing that I am unworthy or not permitted to have abundance.

7. Soccer Injury

Affected area. Right leg.

Source. Fouled in a soccer game, causing him to miss his championship high school season and lose a scholarship.

Guidance.

- I forgive myself for believing my life was over when I was injured.
- I forgive myself for believing my opportunity to be successful was ruined.
- I forgive myself for believing that the other player ruined my life.
- I forgive myself for judging myself for getting hurt.
- I forgive myself for believing that if I heal I will loose the attention I need to make up for not being a soccer star.

8. Loss of Stuffed Bunny

Affected area. Right leg, etheric and emotional body.

Source. As a toddler, his parents were both professionals working for the government foreign service. They moved at least once a year, sometimes leaving their son in someone's care. His stuffed animal became his sense of place and security. On one of the moves, his companion was left behind. He had no one to feel close to and talk to. He decided he would never have support, a place in life, or a home, and that if he did trust, he would be abandoned. His parents (as Father/Mother god) were aloof and unavailable, even though they always provided for his material needs.

Guidance. In this case there are several areas of concern: his relationship to place, belonging, finding his place in the world, finding home in the world and spiritually, and the ability to form an effective alliance with God.

- I forgive myself for believing that I am unlovable.
- I forgive myself for believing I will never have a place in the world.
- I forgive myself for believing that Father/Mother God is unresponsive to me and is not an intimate force in my life.

- I forgive myself for believing I am not allowed to have a home or go home to my spiritual Source.
- I forgive myself for believing that if I form an intimate relationship I will be abandoned.

9. Car Accident

Affected area. Right arm.

Source. As a young man, he was returning home late one night. There had been some drinking, but no one was drunk. The evening had been fun. His friend was driving. The car slid on some ice and crashed, throwing him from the car. The impact broke his arm and he was knocked unconscious. He remembered tying to pull his unconscious friend from the car as it burst into flames, but he could not. What he did not realize was that he was out of his physical body, thus unable to affect his surroundings physically. To the unconscious mind, the imagery was seamless. The inability to save his friend indexed to his broken arm. The pain persisted in his arm even though it healed perfectly.

Guidance. Guided imagery through reliving the event can provide details about what really happened. In this case realizing that he was unconscious and out of his body can relieve the judgment that he failed to save his friend, and release the continuing pain.

- I forgive myself for judging myself because I could not save my friend.
- I forgive myself for believing it was my fault that my friend died.

10. Tooth Fairy

Affected area. Weakness in right shoulder.

Source. At change of teeth a new sense of self is emerging. The event of finding money under your pillow in place of your lost tooth is magical, reassuring and powerful. Metaphorically it is a passage from one developmental stage into another. The child becomes more concretely engaged with life, leaving a more dreamy and imaginal earlier life. In this case, he did not tell anyone that he lost his tooth, so they did not know to play tooth fairy. He awoke to find his tooth and no coin.

Guidance. Intellectually he had realized what happened and had relegated the event to his childhood maturing. However, the occasional weakness in his shoulder persisted, especially when venturing into a situation of uncertain outcome, or when hoping for a good outcome based on uncertain actions. He was also indifferent to celebrations of self like birthdays, awards or promotions.

- I forgive myself for believing I am unworthy.
- I forgive myself for believing magic and reward cannot happen for me.
- I forgive myself for believing that if I expect reward for my accomplishments, I will be disappointed.
- I forgive myself for believing that if I strive for something I really want, I will be disappointed.
- I forgive myself for believing I need to protect myself from being hurt through recognition.
- I forgive myself for believing that recognition and celebration from others is insincere.
- I forgive myself for judging myself because I did not tell anyone about my tooth.

11. Religious Injury

Affected area. There is an energetic channel of connection into the positive matrix of the light and sound.

Source. In a past life, he witnessed the crucifixion and believed that all hope was lost. That the Christ was gone and he was forever abandoned. This is a strange twist in which one believes there is a Christ, yet he is personally abandoned or misled.

Guidance.

- I forgive myself for believing that I am abandoned and betrayed by the Christ and that I can never have a spiritual connection.
- I forgive myself for believing I can never go home and must serve through shame.
- I forgive myself for believing I am doomed to wander through eternity, even though I serve God and do good works.
- I forgive myself for believing I have lost my chance for salvation.
- I forgive myself for believing I was lied to by the Christ and that the teachings and practices he taught are a lie.

DISCOVERY

Distortion in the field takes many forms, and further experience will reveal further types and variations. Because of this we must always embrace new discovery that at any time may completely change how we understand Noetic Field Balancing.

Generic Self Forgiveness

Over the years certain themes evolve with almost all of us. I call these themes "generic self-forgiveness".

These are:

1. For doubting myself and not trusting my life (Solar Plexus).
2. For believing I don't belong in my life or have a place in the world (Feet).
3. For any oath, pledge, agreement, contract or initiation that I took in any place, time, circumstance or dimensions with anything or anyone that was for less than the highest good.

Entities and Attachments

Entities and attachments are often present in the energy field because of predisposing behaviors, beliefs and judgments held by the individual. Recreational drug use is a common one with the use of substances such as alcohol, marijuana, cocaine, heroin, meth, etc., there is an abdication of self, a giving over of one's authority to the substance. This ranges from giving over with a spiritual intent, to just wanting to get out of one's life because it is too frightening or painful, to becoming addicted to the sensation. A good book to look at in this area is *Spiritual High*, by John-Roger.

It is not surprising that so many people in our society seek relief through medication. It is as if there is a zeitgeist that feeds itself through promoting a societal hypnotism that drugs can solve everything. Fortunately, there is an increasing awareness that mental, emotional, dietary and spiritual patterns influence the health and well being of our bodies. When we abdicate our authority, other entities feel they have a right to express or take over our consciousness. From that perspective, as the person works on the patterns that resulted in the invitation, the entities are often structured out of the aura.

There is no longer a welcome for them. However, if an entity is pushed out without changing the condition that let it in, the problem can become worse. The opening will remain, and worse can enter.

Attachments may also be ancient, resulting from past life encounters or agreements. They can take the form of curses, thought forms that control one's volition for a purpose, or a pledge or initiation into a system or force that was for less than the highest. As these stories become conscious, the blocking energy often releases. Often there is need of forming a self forgiveness statement in the same way as for a current situation. Time has no bearing. Some of these impinging forces say that they have a right to control the person because of past agreements. That may have been so then, but not now. The person may forgive him/herself for past agreements, or for believing that by binding themselves to a being or consciousness, they could get what they needed. Sometimes you have to command through the Holy Spirit that the impinging force understand that they no longer have a claim and must leave, and that this be done for the highest good.

On occasions, you, as practitioner, can check and see if it is for the highest good to just remove an entity. Vianna Stibel describes a great approach in her book *Go Up and Work With God*. She instructs the practitioner to go up and connect with God and command that the entity be cleared and returned to whence it came. She calls them *waywards*. You can find the reference on line at www.thetahealing.com.

Transpersonal Blocks

I call these blocks *transpersonal* because they are not held in place by a personal judgment. They are a geometric form or code based on *cultural patterns, folk souls, zeitgeist, implants,* or *genetic lineage*. These patterns may require self-forgiveness, but, for the most part, they release through awareness and witness. Sometimes they require a directed energy push, a directed breath by the client, touch, or transcendental help. In any case, balancing these types of distortions is very difficult if the practitioner is unable to reach an extremely high vibration or spiritual alignment. For the client to clear them, the same elevation is required. A state of witness makes possible Divine aid. For most of us, that is what we do to transform these patterns. There is some solace in the generalization that if you can perceive it, you can assist in clearing it.

Chapter Nine

EXPERIENCE OF NOETIC BALANCING

Epiphany describes the experience of transformation through Noetic Balancing and therapy. It is the moment when forgiveness or a change of heart invites the Light to touch the trauma. At that moment the client experiences an emotional movement and insight of the kind that releases the old structures and constructs new ones.

According to Webster's Electronic Dictionary & Thesaurus, "epiphany" is defined in literature as the moment in the story when the plot is revealed. In liturgy, it is an appearance or manifestation of a deity. Epiphany is a Christian festival, observed on January 6, commemorating the manifestation of Christ to the gentiles in the persons of the Magi; it is the Twelfth Day of Christmas. Epiphany is a sudden, intuitive perception of or insight into reality or the essential meaning of something, often initiated by some simple, commonplace occurrence. Epiphany is a literary work or section of a work presenting such a moment of revelation and insight.

Epiphany may be applied to the experience of Noetic Balancing in every sense of its definition. As the coming of the Light, the epiphany unfolds when invited by the therapeutic context. One aspect of the context, of course, is the block or energy distortion. Others are the intention to transform, the practitioner, and the field of energy created by the intention of the client, focus of the practitioner, and spiritual presence. Within this context, the focus holds attention on the point of concern and the orientation held by the practitioner. The epiphany emerges through the convergence of these dimensional forces. As above, so below.

The following case statements were obtained through a written follow-up survey of clients' experience of Noetic Balancing. These examples reported by clients are touching, beautiful, and inspiring. They demonstrate the place of Noetic Balancing in our lives and illustrate the scope of truly holistic learning and the power of our relationships to heal and teach through our collegial relationship with God. Through out this book, I have called this "God-field" the *noetic field* because, as we experience it, it is universal, intimate, completely loving and intelligent. *Noesis* is the personal experience of epiphany within the *noetic field*. As we are present in the moment, our life is an epiphany. Later in this chapter, I included additional research on the *experience of noesis*.

Case One

The practitioner made me feel very safe and nurtured. At one point, I was very concerned about going deeper. The practitioner sensed this and made a statement that made me feel safe enough to let go to a pretty deep level of myself.

A trusting rapport must develop so that deep communication can develop. This communication is often unspoken. The aura itself is intelligent, and contact with it in a framework of safety can be sufficient to balance.

During the . . . balancing, I had numerous emotional and physical responses. In the beginning, I worked to quiet the chatter in my mind. I began to feel myself letting go. At that point, I began to feel very emotional—lots of grief, some relief was coming up. My right arm began to ache quite a bit also. This cleared by the end of the balancing. Toward the last third of the balancing, I felt both very present and aware of my body and also very expanded to the point that I felt out of my body.

She needed to be deeply seen and touched spiritually in a physical context. The energy touch opens a reservoir of spiritual potency and healing much like coming home within oneself.

The one specific experience, which came up most powerfully during my . . . balancing was an old issue with my mother in which my admiration of my mother was misunderstood and actually caused my mother to lash out at me. [As a child] I had cut off my little white undershirts so that I would be able to look like my mother . . . . She found them and punished me severely, only able to see that I was destroying things. I had been very deeply hurt by this experience which happened when I was between five and seven years old. I was, during the balancing, able to see the cuteness of myself as a child trying to emulate my mother. I was also able to truly forgive my mother for only seeing what she did and attacking who I was and the love and modeling of her that I was expressing. I felt a sense of relief.

Often, key moments highlight the session. These moments often symbolize the essence of the entire session or metaphorically convey a truth for the life span. The central epiphany brought to light the degree to which she had formulated her idea of womanhood from her mother's perspective. Her mother's action actually taught her to mistrust her womanhood and to doubt the substance and worth of her feminine nature. Her admiration can now turn inward to her soul, and her self-forgiveness release the judgments of a rejected, unworthy self.

I feel that since my balancing, I have more clarity about the core issues that are needing to change. I feel that I am more aware of what "on track" feels like for me. I feel more connected to my internal guidance. Although, this was not the case for the first few days after the balancing, when I felt way out of balance and almost reactive.

During and around the time of my . . . balancing, I had been dealing pretty strongly with issues . . . . These thoughts have been kicking around within me for some time. They have come to a head since the . . . balancing. It feels as though things are a bit accelerated as a result of the balancing.

When our energy field comes into balance as a result of noetic therapy the effects are varied and subtle. Core structuring beliefs are changed, and confusing patterns released. Our greater alignment can also be an invitation for new challenges to present themselves. Issues that seemed at bay will come to a head. Centering in a new way signals a readiness to engage the issues in life more strongly; so, as she said, "Things are a bit accelerated."

Case Two

I liked the overall experience I had of my practitioner . . . . There were a few times when I felt he was coaxing me into a certain response that wasn't really my experience. We were able to reach a "common ground" of sorts without too much difficulty.

My recollection of the balancing is that I experienced great relaxation and calmness. I felt a tingling sensation in both my neck and coccyx at different times. The only strong emotional feelings came towards the end when I thought about my grandfather and the special relationship we had.

In this case, there were moments of tension that required the practitioner and the client to find some common ground. A practitioner must be careful not to try too hard to help the client. This eagerness can color the practitioner's perception. It can also create a subtle tension that makes it difficult for the client to be at ease.

I had mixed feelings about the forgiveness exercises. Over the last eight to ten years, I have done a good deal of work around many issues from my childhood and teens. To delve back into them was okay for me . . . . though I sometimes feel as if it's just rehashing or recycling stuff I've come to peace with. Why draw attention to areas I've let go of? Like I said though, I chose the responses, so I assume there's still something left in them for me.

Sometimes the simplicity seems too mundane. Events emerge that we thought we had settled. Yet the approach is to provide focus and accept what is presented as important by the inner noetic wisdom of the client.

The most powerful part for me was toward the end when the practitioner asked me about the special places or havens I had as a child. I especially felt moved when I remembered my mother's father and the special times we shared when I was quite small. I was asked to think of five places that were sacred (my word) to me at four and five years old. Then I was asked to bring the self from those places together and join them inside me. I believe that's a process I'm still doing.

In this case, the client had a lot of experience looking for what was wrong or could be improved upon. This is one of our cultural biases and, in a sense, another form of energy block because it is a belief that keeps us from seeing and implementing healthy patterns in the energy field. The practitioner saw a picture of the client as a youngster in one of his safe places where he would go to nurture himself. Asking about this image, the practitioner began a relationship with the client that precipitated the primary epiphany of this session.

My compassion for myself and others has increased. I've noticed a heightened ability to move into forgiveness more rapidly. As far as my outlook on life, I'm not sure it has changed any viewpoints, per se. I do see the fallibility of we humans a bit differently. The only change in my view of the nature of reality is just a reminder that there is much more in this world than I am able to physically see.

Sometimes we take ourselves for granted and separate from the important parts of ourselves through omission. We leave the helpers of our positive past behind. When they are brought forward and integrated into the present, our present self changes.

Case Three

I sense unconditional love, unconditional positive regard. I feel safe and secure with the practitioner. A space is provided in which I feel accepted. I feel that our conversation brings me to a deeper understanding of what is going on and the deeper spiritual and life lessons involved. It is as if the practitioner takes the facts as I present them and then helps me uncover the truth that lies beneath the facts. I experience the practitioner as truthful and wise and respectful and aligned with the Divine Source.

In this case, the rapport was deep and profound.

I feel very peaceful, poised, and relaxed. I feel attuned to my inner guidance. The confusion and turmoil I felt prior to the session has loosened and I am more able to embrace each moment in consciousness. Obstacles seem to dissipate by the creative spirit working through and in me. I feel clear and I feel myself in my body. I feel more open and loving when I leave the session. I feel connected to myself, more aligned internally and externally. I am in a "flow" and my experiences in the world are more positive. My heart feels open.

The session progressed out of the fullness of the spiritual environment that was established. This person is especially sensitive and attuned to herself as energy. When areas of perception opened, streams of images would flow forward allowing her to spontaneously merge the energy field of forgiveness with the distorted patterns and thereby transform them.

One of the most powerful experiences occurred when the practitioner gave me the thought that the abandonment and betrayal that I experienced early in life is a metaphor for my own self-betrayal and self-abandonment. I never connected to my parents' heart. They never accepted who I was. In order to have some semblance of relationship, I had to become the person they wanted me to be. That was self-betrayal. I was trained not to trust my unconscious. Everything I did had to meet an external standard. The question I asked myself was: Can I love according to my inner truth and not betray myself? Am I willing to let go of fear and resentment and whatever else is contrary to God's nature in me? Under my fear lies the pain of knowing that what I need is loving warm connection with others. What I realized was that I needed to make space for self-love to come in. Self-love comes from not abandoning and betraying myself. This requires daily practice. It means giving up the role of victim, releasing the negative thoughts that lurk in the dark recesses of my mind and reframing them in positive ways and transforming them. It means choosing my thoughts wisely, choosing what I want to experience. This experience has taught me about self responsibility and about experiencing the powerful Source of life that is within me. It is teaching me to connect to the God within me.

Having an aura that is highly sensitive and attuned to the subtleties of the environment in which one lives can also be confusing. A challenge for this person is to learn how to have sensitivity in a way that is not so vulnerable to the forces around her.

I recognize my oneness with Spirit. During [the] balancing, I became still and I realized the jumble of thoughts that are running through my mind. By developing a regular meditation practice, I find my stillness again and learn to let go and let God flow through me. I try to use the meditation. I am finding more good in the world, and I am aware that every person is an evolving soul. I am learning to be true to my own thoughts, and to penetrate more deeply into my consciousness. I am consciously developing my capacity to love, forgive, and be compassionate. I discovered I had a piece of the Divine in me, but I must admit that I am not in a place where I constantly sense the presence of God. There are days were I feel separated from the Source of my love.

In her case, the epiphany came when she realized she had no sense of place, no space for her to be here. As she connected to her inner place of spiritual legitimacy, the cloak of abandonment could lift and she could take her place in her life.

I have learned that my healing is in my heart, mind, spirit. That it may not be physical. I am aware that no matter what happened in the past, I am not bound by previous patterns, emotional reactions, or my health challenges. During aura balancing, I feel my wholeness and have been given the understanding that peace and love are what is true. My hardships are my gifts. Aura balancing is helping me to clear away limited beliefs about myself. This created a space for healing to take place.

In this case, the feeling is a course correction. To feel the separation, she must do so from a felt reference point of alignment or connection. This is true for most of us. When we are numb to or feel disconnected from our alignment, there is greater cause for concern.

Case Four

The way the client experiences the practitioner is very important. When clients feels safe, trusting and cared for, the basic self will readily open the unconscious mind to the practitioner.

I found the practitioner to be very gentle and grounded. I felt safe with her. She was also very clear with a loving presence.

Through the refinement and depth of focus of the practitioner, a deep intimacy develops with the client that can be structural in its impact.

I found the . . . balancing process to be very precise and thorough. It felt as if I had surgery. And the process was a powerful tool to articulate the body, spirit, and mind. It was very simple, yet deeply profound.

In another session, a client described the balancing as having a greater intensity in his connective tissue than her Rolfing sessions. This is interesting in that in Noetic Balancing there is no physical touching.

The entire experience was life-changing for me. To separate out one experience from the other, for me, would be like making a hole in a spider's web. Thematic threads of responsibility for self and others, abandonment and betrayal, and self-trust and speaking my truth ran through the entire session.

I have worked on all of these issues, but somehow during the session I was able to relive these experiences deeply and vividly beginning at a traumatic experience at age four and understanding how these themes have continued to play out in my adult life.

Her epiphany helped her touch into a deeper level of her Holiness and realize a greater depth of healing. The experience of epiphany helped her appreciate the synchronicity in her life and embrace her opportunity to open a new chapter.

I see now that this is a transitional life for me. I have learned and lived the above experience fully. The time has come for me to begin living from my self—my soul—rather than from my pain and suffering. I leave in a few days on a two month pilgrimage to Scotland and England. Interesting, it's the one month "anniversary" of my . . . balancing.

I feel much freer, energetically lighter. I feel more in touch with my emotional needs. Energetically, I feel "smoother" like there are less openings or wounds to be hooked into. I feel very clear so that I can feel the motivations of others in my body

It has been almost a month and I feel much lighter. I feel a greater ease facing issues, almost as if they are being handled for me. A much clearer and profound contact with my soul. I feel connected to God, my soul and my body. I am aware of a deep peace that is always with me no matter how chaotic it is around me. I find it easier to be myself and to be honest with myself and to speak my truth with others. I am aware of making different choices and the difference between how this feels and how it feels when I slip into old patterns. It's much easier to choose something new and to feel okay with the new feeling.

Case Five

The practitioner begins by centering (aligning with Spirit, focusing on the divine nature of the client, and asking for spirit's energy field of unconditional love). The practitioner moves into an altered state, which strongly presents a characteristic goodness, love, and attentiveness, excluding everything outside the therapy room. In these circumstances, the client's sense of the practitioner can be colored by her own qualities.

Present, gentle, supportive, confident—maybe a bit anxious, competent. Trusting of the work. Very sweet.

My emotional responses felt much more charged or intense than the betrayal might suggest. As I was describing my experience, I felt the areas that were activated were holding the emotional charge for many, many such actual events or instances and they were not only my experiences but a collective experience, especially the feminine as being dismissed abused, wounded, ignored, devalued, shamed, abandoned, and killed. It felt archetypal.

She has a quality of soul that allows her to serve a greater arena of healing humanity. This is true for many of us. In this case, the relationship is accentuated. The epiphany contains the awareness of the magnitude of what she is participating in, in the greater field of humanity and spiritual service. Through the mystery of her own evolution, her personal karma reflects the archetypal journey of all of us.

Towards the end of the balancing, I began to feel an effervescent, bubbling, sparkling sensation that felt as if something were dissolving or being released. I then felt as if I knew the true nature of reality in my cells, not separated from anything or anyone. But before that, I was feeling like I was going to die because the energy in my heart was getting so intense. Then, after the balancing, I felt as if I had been time-traveling for a long time—very far. I felt as if this altered state was like a shamanic journey. I went somewhere far away for a long, long time. It was more a sense of timelessness, actually. During the balancing, I felt a lot of pain in my spine; and afterwards, the rest of the day, I had intense pain in my right shoulder and felt rather sick. The next day I was okay.

The balancing enhanced my outlook and the way in which I perceive the nature of reality—as connected to a divine Source. No difference between inner and outer. Also an anchor for the archetypal feminine.

After two weeks, I feel things are still shifting, but beginning to settle. I normally have a lot of physical pain, especially around my spine, from the bottom up, which has sometimes felt more intense and structurally unstable. Just shifting around a bit more than normally happens.

This is her service. A challenge for her is moving her identification of self from personalization of humanity's wounds, to herself as a serving soul who is not defined by what she is serving.

Case Six

The practitioner's initial prayer for alignment with truth, purity of intention for the highest good, and gratitude for the higher powers that wish to be present to help, gave me a sense of being in sacred space for our time together. The practitioner remained impeccably mindful of these initial intentions through each phase of the balancing. He had the humility to serve and guide with a neutral, open mind, not with the glamour of personal power. I really felt his caring for my highest good.

I also particularly cherish some guidance about feelings that came through my practitioner. When I said that I often get too excited about my feelings and that I should be cooler, calmer, he said, "Why not be warmer towards your feelings and welcome them? Feelings are your friends." I felt comfort from these words. Rather than trying to push away and subdue my feelings, I can welcome them as being the helpful messengers that they are.

Feelings are information rather than a source of truth. The information they give us through feeling good, bad, or uncomfortable is important. They are not our adversary. We are prone to attack how we feel instead of paying attention to what those feeling are trying to tell us. The reforming of her feelings changed her consciousness.

Through the energy clearing and self-forgiveness in [the] . . . balancing, I am aligned with the essential kindness of reality. I realize that I am having a perfect life, falls and all. All of my sufferings and joys have served to awaken me to my wholeness.

Throughout the balancing process, the experience of grace is enhanced. The realization that one's life is the right path to fulfillment is a form of grace in itself.

While receiving [the] . . . balancing, I experience gentle presence in moments. By bringing loving awareness to all levels of my being, I allow divine grace to flow unimpeded. Insights and understanding for which I am ready come forth.

During the two weeks after my first aura balancing, I realized how the heaviness from a certain sadness and loss that I had been experiencing for several months was lifting. Although the psychologist I had seen for ten sessions had deepened my understanding of the issues, the . . . balancing was the essential catalyst to really move and clear the sadness and loss and bring true healing.

The epiphany is gradual, seeping in through her vulnerability to the process and the strengthening of her alignment with grace.

During my first session, the practitioner helped me deeply experience the six, ten, and sixteen year old girl in me who felt hurt during specific painful incidents. I was able to love and forgive her for judging herself, that she was somehow wrong or bad for feeling hurt. Now, when I start to feel hurt and to heavily judge myself for it, I can quickly go back to the little girl in the specific time and place when she formed excess self-judgment and reassure her now with my greater understanding and love. Thus I am able to quickly release myself from old patterns and live in the understanding and loving kindness that are my true self.

Two more . . . balancings (two weeks apart) further enriched my healing. Now, six months later, I notice how my work with people, meditation, and journaling continue to be deepened by the doors that opened for me during those three sessions.

The practitioner used a technique of time traveling, described earlier, in which our self-of-now can minister to a particular past self that needed us. The client continued to use this technique to support and realign herself in difficult moments.

CLINICAL NOESIS

With the reading of *Eyes Made of Soul* as a back drop, I would like to include excerpts from a Master of Arts thesis by Ana Pérez, a graduate of the Noetic Balancing Practitioner Program. Her research topic was the *experience of noesis*. The thesis title is: *Clinical Noesis: the Therapeutic Experience of Transcendence in Noetic Field Therapy*.

> "Western psychology has done little to understand and cultivate the transformative power of noesis. Noesis is direct and instantaneous knowledge that surpasses previous knowing. As many are aware, direct experience of what is felt or believed to be truth is an invaluable tool for personal change, transcendence, and even possibly human evolution. The focus of this study is on demonstrating the impact of noesis on the lives of the participants, and introducing a safe, fast, and easy method to access the experience of noesis . . . within a clinical setting for . . . healing of psychological and traumatic disturbances . . . . This heuristic study is an in-depth exploration of the actual experience of noesis in the context of Robert Waterman's Noetic Field Therapy™ (NFT™) [Noetic Field Therapy has been changed to Noetic Balancing.] This approach is principally a psychological intervention model." (Pérez, 2)

To explore this phenomenon, Pérez did a heuristic study of 17 recipients of Noetic Balancing. She primarily used methodology developed by Moustakas (1990) in which she interviewed clients within a few days after their initial session and again at two longer intervals after the session. Themes emerged from the interview material which I have included in the following excerpts along with some of her assessments. Reading the entire document is delightful. I would have loved to include many more elements of the study; however, that would have, in itself, constituted a book in its own right. Perhaps that will happen. The material would certainly be worth broader availability.

Pérez focused on the experience of noeses because it is the moment when transformation occurs in the client's experience. The experience of Noetic Field Balancing is cumulative. The gestalt of clearing several blocks can result in a spontaneous realization or shift in energy. As the limiting beliefs are cleared and trauma is healed, we naturally center, our awareness becomes more resilient in the face of daily challenges, and we become more transcendentally responsive.

The following narration is a synthesis of the respondent interviews. The synthesis of the themes revealed in the interviews is typical of a heuristic study. As in the earlier case studies, I have used italics in place of quotation marks.

For poignancy, I changed the narration to first person. If you like, read it as if it were your experience. You may find an understanding passes to you in the process. You might say that the synthesis voice is in the *collective first person*. The narration follows the sequence of a balancing session.

As the experience happened, the knowing began to integrate into my body. The pain stopped where it started and there was a breathing in my body; my hands released electricity, heat and cold; my body flooded with energy, and I became aware that I was no longer in an ordinary state. The felt bodily shifts and sensations accompanying this accessing of new information signaled the integration of the experience into my body. This release brought to mind the image I saw once in a video at a Peter Levine lecture of a bear in the wild naturally de-traumatizing. It had been shot with a pellet to put it to sleep for a routine medical examination. As the bear was recovering consciousness, it discharged a high level of energy with shaking, twitching, and jerking movements. This is how an animal of prey naturally heals itself, unlike humans who retain the residual energy in their bodies in the form of a trauma.

My body resonated with the truth of my experience; it was an integrated, holistic knowing, down to the very fiber of my being. What I knew only as a concept or an abstraction was now definitely and ultimately real. I was amazed at how easily and quickly my subconscious issues surfaced to the forefront. I was stunned by the sharp awareness of limiting patterns, beliefs, self-judgments, and their connection to past or present experiences.

Minutes later after the peak of my experience, I began to settle, get more grounded or centered. At first, I felt spacey, not quite in my body yet, but still very aware of it. I felt the height of ecstasy. [Other times I] simply felt happy, energized, and motivated. A peacefulness invaded me. I was relaxed and calm. One of the first things I noticed was an expanded awareness. There was a presence, a mental clarity; my senses were heightened, and my intuition was sharp. I felt gratitude for my experiences and my learning. My relationship to myself was changed. Whether I realized what shifted or not, I had a felt-sense that I [was now seeing] my issues through different eyes, through "eyes of soul," as Waterman (1999) says.

For the next few days the shifts continued to integrate, I experienced fluctuations in my physical and energetic bodies and a range of emotions, sometimes very intensely. My dreams during this time were vivid and reflected the issues I was working on or that were stirred up by the experience.

During this time I experienced mood swings, anger at patterns, agitation, [and at times I was] very energized, motivated, joyful and relaxed. By the end of this integration period, the balancing of the energy field was complete and the bodily shifts and emotional upheavals had settled down for the most part. However, what remained was an expanded consciousness, feeling of presence, mental clarity, and calm. I was seeing the world through different lenses.

During this interval and persisting over the next five to six months, I was more aware of my behaviors. I was able to detach from my issues and see my patterns with greater clarity as a non-judgmental observer. The charge around the issue had lessened and I could see that there are more choices available to handle a situation. I began to take charge of my life and make better choices. I responded more instead of reacting to situations. My behaviors and responses were more integrated, whole and automatic as well. I was not run as much by my emotions nor was I cut off intellectually from my heart, from my emotions.

Having released self-judgments, my self-concept and self-esteem increased. I was more comfortable in the world being just who I was. I embraced life, relationships and situations increasingly in a more full-body way. I was less fearful, more empowered and assertive in relationships. There was less need to defend myself. As I judged myself less, I judged others less as well. My partner and co-workers noticed my changes. An increased inner focus was continuing to help me maintain my personal boundary with others and previously difficult situations.

Months after the balancing, I found that I could not recall what transpired during the balancing. It appears that the experience had integrated fully into my daily experience ... But as I was reminded of what I said a few months earlier, it come back into my awareness, sometimes quite vividly. I was usually amazed at how the shifts I experienced then have persisted; how certain things have improved in my life; some goals came into fruition; and necessary changes were undertaken in relationships and my career. My felt-sense was more expanded and aware; I continued to feel more centered, grounded, relaxed, safe, and secure. My behaviors were more spontaneous and integrated.

The realization that the universe is vast had given me a sense of sacredness. An insight arouse suddenly, followed by another, and then another an hour later. It didn't seem to stop. It was more natural to trust my intuition .... I may even apply some of the tools I learned at the balancing to heal myself. I began to notice that I had one foot in one world and one in another, at the same time feeling more present than ever.

Pérez then commented on the narration.

I reflected on the core themes and qualities of the experience of noesis arrived at by way of heuristic inquiry; I can't help but to notice a parallel between this process, the experience of noesis itself, and a Russian "doll within-a-doll". When I made this analogy to my faculty advisor, she told me that grandmothers presented these dolls to their grandchild at birth showing the continuance of the family lineage. The seed is there for generations to come, she said. It makes sense. As you explore the first layer or doll, you find that the doll has given "birth" to another doll underneath, followed by a series of smaller dolls within dolls until the last tiny doll is visible. In an analogous way the process of heuristic examination helps unveil the essential thematic structures and themes one doll at a time, one understanding giving birth to the next until the core is revealed. So it was with the experience of noesis within the structure of Noetic Field Therapy. With each experience, I uncovered an understanding, leading to yet another layer of awareness, until I reached the core of self-realization. Each doll gives way to yet another as the truth of my nature is revealed to me. With each transformation of a self-judgment, I got closer to the core. (Pérez, 3-8)

At one point the client synthesis revealed a comparison to other energetic and psychological therapies experienced. Again, the *collective client*.

When I compare NFT to mainstream approaches to psychotherapy or counseling that I have experienced, in general, I view it as faster, more direct, more powerful, and more effective. One of the major elements missing in counseling that I experienced with the aura balancing was a connecting back to the Source. In comparison to traditional talk therapy, I was stunned by how strongly the issues come up with the balancing.

Even the cognitive-based therapies that promise rapid change fall short of the process of NFT, in my opinion. The shifts experienced with the balancing were direct, fast and permanent. In other words, once the shift took place, I was just different because of it. I transcended to a new level of being in the world around as my relationship to my issue had changed. There was no need to keep going over it over and over to keep reinforcing my mind like affirmations until my subconscious would eventually believe it and made a shift . . . It's really hard to put into words. It's just a pleasure. I get really impatient with a lot of types of therapies. Like I am just wasting time; it's not fast enough for me.

Compared to some Past Life Regression Therapy I had, . . . the transformation was more immediate and in in my face with NFT. In addition, instead of feeling exhausted and having to go lock myself up in my room, after a past life session, I wanted to share my happiness with others after an NFT session. And in comparison to Holotropic Breathwork, I could address [and] clear many more issues in just one NFT session.

NFT was different compared to other [types of] energy work that have a psychological and verbal component; it was more succinct. It was a specific technique that already had the energy clearing tied in with the verbal work because of the technical structure of the noetic field and the chakras.

When compared to other energy or shamanic work I had practiced, it was at least as powerful. As a practitioner of some other forms of energy work (e.g., Therapeutic Touch, Polarity Therapy, Reiki, and acupressure), I find the application of NFT was only slightly different. In spite of the reservations I had with NFT's verbal interventions in conjunction with the energy component, I . . . noticed that I had a powerful Aha! during the balancing.

In most instances, I perceived the numerous revelations to add value to the modality's effectiveness as a tool for change and even transcendence. The knowledge conveyed to me had a continuous effect in opening the closed doors of my perception. (Pérez, 130-133)

Pérez reflects:

This . . . study demonstrates the value inherent in the use of noesis in a clinical setting as a transformative and transcendent technique. It also illustrates the significance of . . . Noetic Field Therapy balancing for an elegant and undemanding induction of noesis. There are many implications here for the field of psychotherapy and society. I believe these findings represent a new paradigm for both individual psychological health and societal wellness. As the beliefs that bind us are transformed into more life-affirming convictions congruent with our true essence, we may one day transcend as a species and live joyfully in peace. (Pérez, 168)

FULL MEASURE

This book arose from forty years of researching, practicing and teaching *Noetic Balancing* and exploring the application of *ancient wisdom* to modern therapy and living. While I was continuing to present classes and conduct sessions in Noetic Therapy, I was founding and developing Southwestern College in Santa Fe, New Mexico, as an accredited graduate school for educating therapists. The challenge at Southwesten College was one of translating the *ancient wisdom* and experience of *Noetic Balancing* into the counseling curriculum in a appropriate way.

As Pérez discovered in her research, when we apply the teaching of Noetic Balancing to our own health and well being and the health and well being of others, we expand our perception of life and who we are. We embrace a new way of participating in life and expressing who we are. We realize that service is intrinsic to who we are.

In the normal passage of our ego, our lives deliver to us the experiences that enable the soul to actualize itself. This is the realm of therapeutic transformation. On the dimension of our internal frontiers, the territory of the soul, we journey inward into essence, into Source. This journey activates the strength of our spiritual presence. By so doing, we open inward doors to the realms of self and God. This has impact in the world. It pushes to the surface our unresolved issues and forgotten creation. The outer and inner challenges increase and intensify.

As if one mirror was not enough, during this phase, it can be helpful to have a guide, or witness. As we increasingly trust our Holiness, the stress subsides. It may only take a simple self forgiveness, on any level, dimension or embodiment, for each time that we have chosen away from the experience of our center, or soul, noesis. As the inner light intensifies, we often become calmer. Symptoms of soul-centering are joy, peace, love, enthusiasm, abundance, and liberation. Finally, we invite, or command (not demand) all of the shadows within us on any level or dimension to come forward into the light and dissolve. We take full responsibility for life as a mirror of our own inner life. Through *eyes made of soul* we see life as the interplay of resolved and unresolved expressions of life as a continual encounter with our eternity lived through the actualization and fulfillment of the moment. Millennia of unrequited hopes and dreams enfold and unfold with each breath, each step. Responsibility is not shame and blame. It is the forgiving of self in witness of the shame and blame.

This is our way. It is in the process of living on earth that we come to realize that this incarnation is a deeper movement of life and love. The seeming conflicts belie a deeper Source to our story. The Noetic Balancing continually reinforces the client's ability to reference reality on *living love*. When we speak of *eyes made of soul*, we refer directly to the eye of perception that forms with each breath. As we enhance our ability to reference truth to love, we have the Source we need to correct all distortions and deceptions. When we transform the opportunities of life into soul substance, we increase our ability to see, evaluate and choose from soul. Increasingly, our eyes become *soul eyes*. As it was said in ancient times, "We first look through a glass darkly, then face to face."

We are in a constant relationship with each other, reformulating reality. However, the reality that we experience is referenced to our alignment, our karma, our soul. From the perspective of a therapist, you are reformulating your reality by serving the client. When you meet your client, you meet your unknown self. We begin where we end.

We honor our clients, associates and friends as our forgotten selves. Each one reflects the unmet orphan within us. The one we created through choices and actions that we did not carefully source and embody in *living love*. Now it is time for reconciliation. When someone engages your life as friend or foe, practitioner or client, colleague or competitor, you must consider the magnitude and opportunity that has just appeared in your reality. The simple fact of their existence in your reality is your accountability. You face them within yourself and say, *I am so sorry. I love you. I forgive myself for all the times I have created, promoted or allowed the misunderstanding and judgments reflected in this issue, and I forgive myself for any time my ancestors contributed to similar circumstances.*

In our wholeness, we still exist at the dawn of time making and remaking the decision to live consciously in God or to reach out into life as if we are separate from the one creator, therefore acting as if we believe that we are the Source. For this, we are collaborators with all the strife and conflict that inhabits this world. We are not guilty, as a criminal is guilty, for ours was an act of inexperience. Now, however, there is no excuse. We know better. So, we stand and face all, neither good nor bad. It was I, and through that power all reconciliation is mine.

As a child I puzzled at the story of the crucifixion of Jesus Christ. He first *died* then he *lived again.* I should do as well, or better. As the self I made in the mirror dies, I see anew through *eyes made of soul.*

Ultimately our presence becomes a *cradle of love* holding all life as if it were new-born. We know again that in this moment, just now, all has come around to its origin in our choice.

Appendix One

THE PRACTIONER MYSTIQUE

There is a timeless adage that our eyes are the windows to our soul. The inference being that you could see the person's soul through their eyes, or the lack of its presence. Certainly, we have experienced a soul nexus through eye contact, as well, the chill of eyes that are closed to the soul or those trained to dominate. Soul eyes invite us to a deeper perception and metaphor of life. We can see life through our soul. We sense our soul looking out through our eyes. In the East they have an expression of this called the "Twaji", which is a spiritual transmission that passes through the eye from the soul of the enlightened one. This is true for all of us in at our personal level of grace as we look out from within, through our eyes. At a deeper level, we can see life through our soul. When this occurs, we can see through a multidimensional awareness grounded in unconditional love. When this occurs, our presence becomes our "eyes." As the master said: "When the eye is single, the whole body is filled with Light." We perceive life through the awareness of our presence. Living Love is the nature of the soul. In our evolving self, our physical life increasingly reflects our soul. When our eyes are made of soul, we see through everything. Our presence permeates our perception, translating our reality into grace. Our eyes are made of soul when we awaken as the soul light that we are. This transformation is essential for becoming a truly effective practitioner.

There is an attraction to being one who spiritually knows and serves. I call this the *practitioner mystique*. Historically that mystique has, at times, been distorted to serve political power or self importance. There is a mystery to the understanding of soul centered living, however, our first lesson at the Amenti School is to de-mystify. We reach into our truth and dissolve the illusion. We become more ourselves in the true sense of soul and through that we become better servants of others. The education we offer provides a strong foundation in self and spirit and how to extend that skill into guiding transformation.

Eyes Made of Soul is a manual for students of energy healing. It is required for students in the Amenti School's practitioner program (www.mystery-school.com). It is likely that you found the book first and didn't know about the program. At the Amenti School, we are committed to developing ways to apply ancient wisdom to transforming ourselves as the way to transform our lives, communities and nations. Ancient can, also, mean antiquity. It refers to that wisdom that is primordial within us, innate in our soul. Consider that the strongest direction for your interest in becoming a practitioner is to enroll in our program. You may already be an energy practitioner and consider *Eyes Made of Soul* a sufficient resource. I have been working in this field for forty years. Based on that experience, I recommend our course as an important complement to you understanding and skill.

You can find our curriculum detailed on our web-site (www.mystery-school.com). We are constantly updating this site with new courses in various locations. Many of the courses are taught in Santa Fe, New Mexico, however, we do offer course in other location in the United States as determined by our sponsors. Courses are also available in Europe. The Noetic Balancing Practitioner program requires a prerequisite study. The applicant must take one of two options. One is the completion of Mystery School One, Two and Three. An alternate option for the prerequisite is Spiritual Science One and Two. Another associate plans to offer pre-requisite and practitioner courses on the East coast sometime in 2011, so check the web.

Your interest in *using Eyes Made of Soul* as a personal or professional resource may align with goals other than becoming a practitioner. In that case, the mystery school, or spiritual science, could be invaluable. If you are a teen or young adult, we also have leadership programs based on the same wisdom.

Whether you join us in our classes or not, let this be an invitation for like minded, and hearted, individuals to join in a collegial way. Many individuals and groups are arising from the same soul response to the transformative call of these times. We live in a time of possible fulfillment of a new day for human kind.

Appendice Deux

FRANÇAIS

SCHÉMAS DE L'AURA

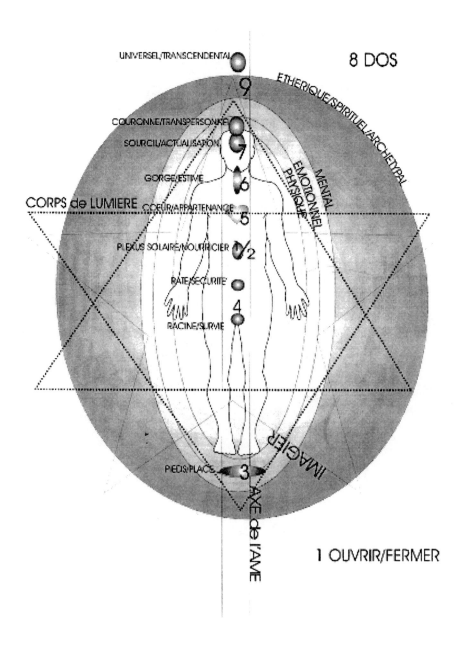

Prière

Père, Mère, Dieu, je te demande ici et maintenant d'être enveloppé par la Lumière du Christ, avec la guidance du Saint Esprit.

Je demande seulement ce qui est pour le plus grand bien de tous ceux qui sont concernés, gardant à l'esprit toutes les destinées sur la planète.

Avec la permission du Christ et du Saint Esprit, je demande la présence et l'assistance de tous les anges, êtres de lumière, maîtres et enseignants qui le souhaitent, pour le bien êtres de tous.

Nous demandons ceci dans l'amour parfait et la compréhension parfait, et nous vous remercions pour ce moment.

Que Ta volonté soit faite.

PROTOCOLE DE LA PRIÈRE

1) Une invitation à s'aligner et à s'abandonner à une puissance supérieure.
2) Engagement intérieur d'impeccabilité.
3) La création d'un espace sacré.
4) Engagement à être dans la dévotion au plus grand bien.
5) Expression de gratitude.

Dialogue Type

Chaque affirmation du dialogue correspond à un chiffre indiqué sur le diagramme. La séquence numérotée indiqué un ordre de progression commençant au chiffre 1 et terminant à 8.

1) Parlez-moi d'un moment de votre vie où vous étiez seul, où vous aviez peur, vous sentiez abondonné ou faisiez l'expérience de culpabilité ou de honte.
2) Parlez-moi d'un moment de votre vie où vous étiez confus (e) ou ne compreniez pas, où vous vous sentiez sans soutien, où vous n'aviez pas de place et n'apparteniez pas.
3) Parlez-moi d'un moment de votre vie où vous avez jugé votre sexualité ou créativité et où vous avez eu du ressentiment ou un besoin de revanche.
4) Parlez-moi d'un moment de votre vie où vous avez eu des regrets où vous vous êtes senti déçu ou trahi ou bien avez essayez de partager votre amour mais n'avez pas pu.
5) Parlez-moi d'un moment de votre vie où vous avez eu de la difficulté à parler ou parce ce que vous avez parlé.
6) Parlez-moi d'un moment de votre vie où vous avez vu ou entendu quelque chose qui était douloureux, perturbant ou effrayant.
7) (L'intervenant est d'habitude silencieux.) Des fardeaux, trahisons ou colères peuvent apparaître.
8) (Intervenant silencieux) Alignement spirituel. Il peut y avoir comme une forme de plafond, indiquant la présence de revanche.,

BIBLIOGRAPHY

Assagioli, R. *Psychosynthesis.* New York: VikingPress, 1974.
Bartlett, R. *The Physics of Miracles.* Oregon: Atria Books, 2009.
Brennan, B A. *Hands of Light: A Guide to Healing Through the Human Energy Field.* New York: Bantam Books, 1988.
Calloway, C. *Psychology for Learning and Teaching.* New York: McGraw Hill, 1976.
Cayce, E. *Auras.* Virginia Beach: ARE Press, 1943.
Hillman, J. *The Myth of Analysis.* New York: Harper & Row, 1972.
—. *The Soul's Code.* New York: Random House, 1996.
Judith, J. *Wheels of Life.* St Paul, MN: Llewellyn Publications, 1995.
Khan, H I. *Spiritual Dimensions of Psychology.* New Lebanon, NY: Omega Press, 1981.
Kit, W K. *The Art of Chi Kung: Making the Most of Your Vital Energy.* Rockport, MA: Element Books, Inc, 1993.
Leadbeater, C W. *Man Visible and Invisible.* Wheaton, IL: Theosophical Publishing House, 1969.
Milarepa. *The Life of Milarepa.* Translated by L P Lhulungpa. New York: Penguin Books, 1979.
Mindell, A. *Dreambody: The Body's Role in Revealing the Self.* Boston, MA: Sigo Press, 1982.
Moustakea, C. *Heuristic Research: Design, Methodology, and Applications.* Newbury Park, CA: Sage, 1988.
Myss, C. *Anatomy of the Spirit: The Seven Stages of Power and Healing.* New York: Harmony Books, 1996.
Pérez, A. M. *Clinical Noesis: The Therapeutic Experience of Transcendence in Noetic Field Therapy.* Dissertation presented to Antioch University McGregor. Santa Fe, NM: 2003.
Pierrakos, J D. *Core Energetics.* Mendocino, CA: Life Rhythm Publication, 1987.

Powers, E. *Auric Mirror.* Alamogordo, NM: Quimby Metaphysical Libraries, 1973.

Quimby, P P. *The Quimby Manuscripts.* Edited by H W Dresser. Secaucus, NJ: The Citadel Press, 1969.

Rama, S, R Bellentine, and S. Ajaya. *Yoga and Psychotherapy.* Glenview, IL: Himalayan Institute, 1976.

Reich, W. *Character Analysis.* New York: Simon & Schuster, 1972.

Stibal, V. *Theta Healing.* Idaho Falls: Roling Thunder Publishing, 2007.

Taylor, K. *The Ethics of Caring: Honoring the Web of Life in Our Professional Healing Relationships.* Santa Cruz: Hanford Mead Publishers, 1995.

Waterman, R D. *Foot Prints of Eternity: Ancient Wisdom Applied to Modern Psychology.* Conshohoken, PA: Infinity Books, 1999, 2006

CPSIA information can be obtained
at www.ICGtesting.com
Printed in the USA
LVOW11s2130260517
535890LV00001B/2/P